GOLDEN RETRIEVERS

Miss Gill, a championship show judge of the breed, had her first Golden Retriever in 1936. Since the war she has owned or bred seven champions, two other challenge certificate winners, and several Field Trial winners. She also bred the only International Dual Champion Golden Retriever ever. She has seven times been awarded the Gold Trophy at Cruft's for the best Golden Retriever winning at trials. In this invaluable book she writes about the care of the Golden Retriever, his looks and his character, giving expert advice and guidance on care, breeding, and training for work and show—everything in fact that the owner of a Golden Retriever needs to know.

JOAN GILL

GOLDEN RETRIEVERS

With a Foreword by
ELMA STONEX

FOYLES HANDBOOKS
LONDON

ISBN 0 7071 0259 6

First published 1962
Reprinted 1972
Reprinted 1973
Reprinted 1975
Reprinted 1976
Reprinted 1978
Reprinted 1979

Published in Great Britain by
W. & G. Foyle Ltd.
125 Charing Cross Road
London WC2H 0EB

Printed and bound in Great Britain
at The Pitman Press, Bath

ACKNOWLEDGEMENTS

The author wishes to extend her grateful thanks to Mrs. Stonex for information on some early dogs, to Mrs. Adlard for typing the manuscript, and to all those who lent photographs.

Contents

List of Illustrations

Foreword

IT WAS a great honour to be asked to write the Foreword for this book. Miss Joan Gill had her first Golden Retriever in 1936, war service in the W.A.A.F. then intervened, but since 1947 when dog activities restarted she has gone from strength to strength in establishing one of the foremost dual-purpose kennels in the breed, and has bred five champions including the only International Dual Champion Golden there has ever been. No one can be better qualified to say what a Golden Retriever should be in every way, and how it should be looked after in all aspects.

I have been asked to say something of the breed's origin on which I have done some research over the last ten years.

Until 1952 this had always been a rather controversial question. Many people had read, and firmly believed in, the story that the breed's originator Sir Dudley Marjoribanks, first Lord Tweedmouth, had bought a troupe of Russian circus dogs at Brighton in 1858 and taken them to Guisachan, his Scottish estate, as gundogs and for tracking wounded deer. It was said that he bred from these dogs and their descendants for a long time, using only a Bloodhound for outcross blood, and occasionally giving puppies to friends. Col. the Hon. W. le Poer Trench of the St. Hubert's kennel, who firmly supported this theory, had in 1883 obtained one or two of these supposedly pure Russian-breds, and photographs of his are something like a pale fawn-coloured Pyrenean Mountain dog. Big and powerful with tremendous coats, they were extremely impressive and handsome, with beautiful heads. At the end of last century my father as a young man frequently shot with Col. Trench, and the latter always took out a brace of these dogs with him.

11

However a good many gundog people thought the Russian story unlikely. They considered that the 'yellow breed' were descended from 'sports', which not infrequently occurred in litters of black Flat or Wavy-coated Retrievers, and in Curly-coats. These sports were generally called liver-colour, but evidently that covered all the sandy shades from pale yellow to brown. (Retrievers only became popular as gundogs in the last half of the nineteenth century. They were first shown in 1864). Which view was the right one might never have been known if Lord Tweedmouth's great-nephew the sixth Earl of Ilchester, historian and sportsman, had not in 1952 published an article in *Country Life* giving details from the former's hitherto unknown kennel records of several different breeds.

Meticulously kept from 1835 to 1890 these gave concrete proof of fact to the origin. There was no mention whatever of any Russian dog, or dogs. The truth was seen to be that in 1865 Lord Tweedmouth bought his first yellow Retriever at Brighton, a dog named Nous, bred by the Earl of Chichester, and that in 1867 he got a Tweed Water-Spaniel Belle, from his cousin Mr. David Robertson, M.P., of Ladykirk on the Tweed. Tweed Water-Spaniels were a fairly rare breed, but several books mention them, and the most concise description is given by 'Stonehenge' in his *British Rural Sports*, where he wrote, 'The Tweedside Spaniel, which resembles a good deal in appearance a small English Retriever of a liver colour'. They were usually curly-coated.

Nous (i.e., Wisdom) and Belle produced four yellow puppies in 1868, at Guisachan, Inverness-shire, which were named Crocus, Primrose, Ada and Cowslip, and were the foundation of the Golden Retriever as a breed. Pictures of all these, except Belle and Primrose, exist, and show them to be remarkably like modern Goldens in type, medium gold in colour and with fairly profuse wavy coats. Some were pretty big, others of quite modern size.

Ada was given to the fifth Earl of Ilchester and founded his Melbury strain, in which to start with black Retrievers were freely used on the yellow.

Cowslip was retained by Lord Tweedmouth, who had a very

advanced scientific approach to dog-breeding for that time. He was clearly determined to make a breed of yellow Retrievers, and through the kindness of his grand-daughter Marjorie, Lady Pentland, in lending me his records I have been able to see exactly how he did it over the following twenty years. Of course many descendants of that first litter were also given to friends and in time found their way all over the country. In all probability their owners crossed the blood with other gundog breeds, but without doubt they all gradually helped to form the Golden Retriever we know today.

The last two yellow puppies Lord Tweedmouth recorded, named Prim and Rose, were born in 1889. Their sire on his sire's side was a grandson of Cowslip through her mating to a red Setter, and on the dam's side he was also her great-grand-son through her earlier mating to a Tweed Water-Spaniel (remember Cowslip herself was half Tweed Water-Spaniel). Prim and Rose's maternal grand-dam was litter-sister to their sire, so they also went back twice to Cowslip on that side. This was unusual line-breeding for those days, but Lord Tweed-mouth had brought in two further out-crosses, a black Retriever as a mate for Cowslip's daughter in 1877, and in 1887 another (a full-brother to the Flat-Coat Ch. Moonstone) which was the sire of Prim and Rose's dam. The latter a black bitch from a litter of ten blacks!

It is known that a sandy-coloured Bloodhound was used somewhere about 1890, but it was evidently after the record-book entries stopped. Lord Tweedmouth died in 1894.

The second Lord Tweedmouth and his cousin the fifth Earl of Ilchester unfortunately kept no kennel records, and few of the 'Yellow Retrievers' they bred were registered, so that it is almost impossible to join the Guisachan descent to the backs of our modern pedigrees. One or two however are known. Notably Conon, who is behind Ch. Heydown Gunner, double great-grandsire of Gilder, whose blood is so largely through the breed today. The biggest link of all came to light when Marjorie, Lady Pentland, lent me a letter written to her by John MacLennan, one of a family of Guisachan keepers. He wrote that the first Viscount Harcourt, of the Culham kennel, one of the first to show the breed, bought his original brace of puppies from a litter MacLennan bred out of a daughter of Lady, a Guisachan-bred bitch owned by the Hon. Archie Marjoribanks, youngest son of the first Lord Tweedmouth. In photographs of Lady taken in 1894 she looks about four or five years old. It is safe to say that Lord Harcourt's dogs, Culham Brass and Culham Copper, born in 1904 and 1908, lie behind practically every Golden there is now.

Another early strain behind most present-day dogs were Mr. W. Macdonald's Ingestre's (about 1904-1915) said to have been started by him from 'a liver Flatcoat bitch'. The well-known ancestress Yellow Nell was out of Ingestre registered parents, bred from unregistered stock, but she has always been said to have been of close Guisachan blood. A number of 'yellows' Macdonald bred, were sired by black Flat-coats.

The Golden Retriever was not given a separate register at the Kennel Club until 1913. Until then they came under the Flat-Coated Retriever heading, and were identifiable only by colour. It is now known that the liver-coloured Flat-Coat winner of the I.G.L. field trial stake in 1904 was sired by Lucifer, an unregistered dog bred by the second Lord Tweedmouth at Guisachan.

Perhaps the odd black spot – I have seen three since 1939, on ribs, shoulder and tail-tip on different dogs – is a reminder of the hard work breed pioneers put into evolving the Golden Retriever in the forty years between 1868 and 1910.

In 1959, only a few months before his death, the late Lord Ilchester, who did the breed such service by bringing the truth of its origin to light, asked me to join him in approaching the Kennel Club for their recognition of the new facts. They approved, and now the way in which Lord Tweedmouth founded the Golden Retriever as a breed is officially recorded each year in Cruft's catalogue.

ELMA STONEX,
Burlands Farm,
Taunton,
Somerset.

Introduction

MY FIRST Golden Retriever was given to me in 1936 as a birthday present. I chose this breed because I thought it was the most beautiful, and I still think so, but it is their delightful character and temperament which has made me a devoted 'Golden' admirer and owner ever since Simon was presented to me all those years ago.

They are essentially a friendly and good tempered breed, but that does not mean that they cannot be trained to be good house dogs. Neither does it mean that they all have exactly the same sort of character. In my own kennel I have firstly the one man type, who is perfectly friendly with other people but remains definitely my dog, and is not completely happy if I'm away. He is the grandson of my first Golden, and is called after him. The first Simon didn't like my being away either, but he got used to it during the war, when I was in the W.A.A.F. I have always found Goldens will adapt themselves to any circumstances.

I had a bitch Ch. Susan of Westley who would go off with anyone who carried a gun. It didn't matter if he was a perfect stranger. If he had a gun she thought he was all right, but she wouldn't go with a stranger without one.

Then there is Ch. Camrose Nicolas of Westley who loves everybody. I really think he would be happy anywhere providing there was someone to make a fuss of him sometimes, and another dog to play with. He greets everyone with a smile. He really does smile, by drawing back his mouth and screwing up his eyes, and if he's really pleased to see you, it broadens to a grin!

Once, at the end of a rather tiring show, he was lying flat-out on his bench asleep, when a friend came along and said

'Hallo Nicky'. He was much too tired to open his eyes, but he waved a paw in the air for her to hold. That is a habit all Goldens seem to have. If you talk to them they nearly always answer by giving you a paw, and attract your attention by putting a paw on your arm. There is never any need to teach them to 'shake hands'.

The retrieving instinct is very strong in almost all Goldens. You will find that when your dog comes to greet you, he will always bring a 'present' in his mouth if he can find one. Susan would fetch a piece of straw from her bed if she couldn't find anything else when I went up to the kennel.

My present house dog, Ch. Simon of Westley, has a favourite black woolly mat, and he always makes a beeline for that if anyone comes. His father, Ch. Camrose Fantango, prefers a cushion, which is so large that he almost falls over it, but I think the favourite 'present' is a shoe, or even a pair of shoes!

If, by this time, you are thinking you had better not have a Golden Retriever after all, because you don't want your belongings carted all over the house, let me hasten to assure you that he can be trained not to touch certain objects. If there is anything you don't want 'retrieved' say 'No' very firmly every time he goes to pick it up and *take* it away from him. The best thing to do is to give him an old shoe, or something similar, of his own, which he can carry about as much as he likes.

I might add that it is rare for large objects like rugs and cushions to be retrieved. It is usually only shoes or gloves, and they are not chewed up, except, of course, by young puppies, but that applies to any breed. It is safer not to leave 'chewable' objects around with puppies when they are teething.

I will tell you a short anecdote about my first Golden. A friend came to spend the evening with us and stayed rather late. She kept saying she must go, but she didn't. After she had said it for about the sixth time, Simon went to the door. I let him out into the hall, and he went straight to the chair where my friend had left her gloves and handbag, picked them up, and took them to her. She took the hint! You think it was coincidence? Perhaps it was, but I prefer to think it was an example of extreme intelligence!

INTRODUCTION

Although many Goldens enjoy their lives purely as pets and companions, they are primarily Gundogs, and are never happier than when working. You may never be able to take your dog out shooting, but you can direct his working instincts into the proper channels and give him a lot of pleasure, and probably yourself as well, by training him on dummies.

The very early breeders took great pains to make Goldens dual purpose dogs, that is dogs who are workers, and are also capable of winning in the show ring.

Nobody did more to put Golden Retrievers on the map in both spheres than the late Mrs. Charlesworth of the Noranby prefix. She had her first Golden in 1906, a bitch without a pedigree, whom she called Noranby Beauty. She was an excellent worker, and had several litters. One of her sons, Noranby Campfire, became the first Golden Retriever Champion.

Mrs. Charlesworth first showed her dogs in 1909, but the previous year Lord Harcourt showed some of his Yellow Retrievers, as they were then called. His prefix was Culham. There was no separate classification for them, as the Kennel Club didn't recognize them officially until 1913. This was the year that Mrs. Charlesworth, aided by a few other enthusiasts, founded the Golden Retriever Club. This Club then drew up the standard of points, which remains the same today except for one small addition. Cream was then barred as a colour, but in 1936 the standard was amended to allow this colour. Lord Harcourt also bred the first dog to win his title at both shows and Field Trials. This was Dual Ch. Balcombe Boy, owned, trained and handled by Mr. R. O. Herman.

The quality of Goldens today is very high, and the photographs in this book are all of post-war dogs, but we owe a great debt to these pioneers, who also included the Hon. Mrs. Grigg (Kentford) and Mr. W. S. Hunt (Ottershaw). They produced, from the early goldens, which were big, heavy, rather slow dogs with long backs and enormous coats, the present day active, fast and short coupled dogs of handy size, while retaining the broad head, good bone and dense water resisting coat.

The breeders of the 1920's and 1930's continued the good work. Fortunately some of them still breed, show and judge the breed and run them in Field Trials. To mention just a few of the principal Kennels of that period between the wars there was the Hon. Mrs. Carnegie, whose Heydown Goldens have many winning descendants today. She actually started in 1916 with Glory of Fyning. Miss Newton Deakin (Tone), Mr. and Mrs. Evers-Swindell (Speedwell), whose first dog became Ch. Cornelius, Mrs. Eccles whose Haulstones still run successfully at Field Trials, Mr. and Mrs. Venables Kyrke (Anningsley) who had a Dual Champion in Anningsley Stingo, Mrs. Cottingham (Woolley), Mrs. H. L. Kirk and her son Mr. R. L. Kirk (Moreton) whose Ch. Michael of Moreton was a true Dual Purpose dog, and sired 7 champions, Mrs. Vernon Wentworth (Donkelve), Mr. Wentworth Smith whose Yelme Dual purpose Kennel is now carried on by Mrs. Wentworth Smith. He owned the famous Gilder, who sired 8 champions and many Field Trial winners. Rev. Needham Davies (Sundawn) who bred Gilder, Mrs. Nairn (Stubbings), whose daughter Mrs. Winston now owns the prefix and Mrs. Stonex (Dorcas). Her Dorcas Bruin gained the first junior warrant ever won by a Gundog (except cockers). His show career was cut short by the war, but he has many winning descendants, including several champions. Mr. and Mrs. Parsons (Torrdale) whose first Golden was Ch. Dukeries Dancing Lady, who has an enormous number of winning descendants. Ch Torrdale Betty won 14 C.C.s and that number hasn't yet been equalled by any other bitch. Mrs. Pilkington (Alresford) whose Alresford Advertiser, a post-war dog, has the highest number of C.C.s ever won by a Golden, Mrs. H. J. Morgan (Weyland), Mrs. Fraser (Westhide), Mrs. and Mrs. Walker (Hazelfax), whose Ch. Hazelgilt just missed his Dual Title. Mr. Jenner (Abbots) had his first Golden in 1917, and was one of the most successful breeders between the two wars. He owned or bred ten champions and four show champions, including Ch. Michael of Moreton and Ch. Dukeries Dancing Lady.

Goldens gradually increased in popularity and in 1938 the registrations at the Kennel Club totalled 1,073. This meant stiffer competition and by the efforts of the breeders mentioned and many others, type became much more even. The standard was high in 1939 when war broke out and placed severe restrictions on shows, but not on breeding. There were no championship or open shows, but sanction shows with a 25 mile radius was allowed. This restriction of competition and the demand for puppies later in the war resulted in much indiscriminate breeding by people who were not interested in maintaining the correct type.

Fortunately for the breed, and for those of us who either started, or restarted after the war, some of the pre-war breeders had kept their strains going and had maintained the high standard reached in 1939. These good dogs won and gradually the poor specimens seen at the early post-war shows disappeared from the ring. Today evenness of type and quality throughout the breed, whose registrations for 1960 reached 2,551 (14th out of over 100 breeds) has never been higher. To illustrate this I cannot do better than to quote the well-known Gundog authority, Mr. H. S. Lloyd (of 'Ware' cocker fame), who wrote in *Our Dogs* after Cruft's 1961, where Goldens had a record entry of 516 made by 242 dogs, the following passage: 'Golden Retrievers have been bred better to type during the last ten or fifteen years than almost any other breed and today it is wonderful to see the classes of upwards of a score all showing little or no variation in size, colour, coat and action. I take my hat off to the tremendous amount of hard work put in by these people.'

This is high praise, and when to this is added the fact that ever increasing numbers of Golden owners are taking every opportunity to work their dogs and run them in Field Trials, the future of the breed would seem very bright indeed.

CHAPTER 1

The Standard

THE FOLLOWING is the Golden Retriever Standard:

General Appearance: Should be of a symmetrical, active, powerful dog, a good level mover, sound and well put together, with a kindly expression, not clumsy or long in the leg.

	Maximum Points
Head: Broad skull, well set on a clean and muscular neck, muzzle powerful and wide, not weak-jawed good stop. *Eyes:* Dark, and set well apart, very kindly expression, with dark rims. *Teeth:* Even, neither under nor overshot	20
Ears: Well proportioned, of moderate size and well set on	5
Nose: Should be black	5
Colour: Any shade of gold or cream, but neither red nor mahogany. The presence of a few white hairs on chest permissible. White collar, feet, toes, or blaze should be penalized	10
Coat: Should be flat or wavy with good feathering, and dense, water-resisting undercoat	5
Feet: Round and cat-like, not open or splay ...	10
Fore-legs: Straight, with good bone.	10
Hind-legs: Strong and muscular, with good second-thighs, stifles well bent	10
Hocks: Well let-down...	10

Tail: Should not be carried too gay or curled at the
tip   5

Body: Well-balanced, short coupled and deep
through the heart. Loins should be strong, ribs deep
and well sprung. Shoulder should be well laid back
and long in the blade   25

Total ...   115

*Note: The average weight for dogs in good hard condition
should be: Dogs 60–70 lb.; Bitches 56–60 lb. Height at
shoulder: Dogs 22 in. to 24 in. Bitches 20 in. to 22 in.*

The scale of points was inserted, when the Golden Retriever
Club first drew up the Standard, as a rough guide to the
relative importance of its different Sections. When judging one
does not award marks to each dog and then add them up to
see who is the winner. To start with, no marks are allotted to
general appearance amd movement, and both of these are of
great importance.

To the beginner the standard probably needs some explana-
tion, so I will enlarge upon it. The Golden Retriever should be
a well-balanced dog, that is, every part in proportion to the
other. He should be alert and on his toes, as befits a working
dog. When moving, he should have a long and powerful stride,
his feet and hocks straight, turning neither in nor out. A dog is
cow-hocked if his hocks turn inwards, and sickle-hocked if
they turn outwards. If he moves with his front feet turned
inward, he is said to be 'pin-toeing', and he is moving 'close
behind' if his hind legs, usually from the hocks downwards,
are too close together.

His head, though broad, should not be coarse. It should
have a chiselled, clean cut appearance with the muzzle or fore-
face in proportion to the skull in breadth, depth and length.

The length from occiput to eyes should be approximately the same as from the eyes to the tip of the nose. His eyes can be any shade from mid-brown to very dark brown. A light eye seldom gives the correct expression, which at one moment may be soulful and sad, the next humorous, and then alert and eager, but always kindly, and never hard.

The ears shouldn't be too thick and heavy, or set on too low like a spaniel's. Neither should they be too high, which is inclined to spoil the expression. They should be set on about level with the eyes.

The standard says that the teeth should be level, which may give the impression that the top and bottom teeth should meet exactly. However, the generally accepted correct mouth for Goldens and all other Gundogs is the scissor bite, in which the top front teeth touch and slightly overlap the bottom.

The jet black nose, lips and eye rims of the Golden are most attractive, and that is the ideal to aim at, but many of them get a distinctly 'rusty' look in winter. This doesn't matter very much, but the really pink nose that is occasionally seen does detract considerably from the dog's appearance.

The front legs should be quite straight, with both elbows and feet turning neither in nor out. A puppy will often turn his feet out slightly, but with exercise to strengthen the pasterns, this will often be corrected.

The hind legs should have well-bent stifles. The stifle is the joint between the femur and tibia and corresponds to the human knee. These bones should be long, while the bone between hock and foot should be short. A straight stifle cannot give sufficient length and power of stride, even though the hind legs are well muscled.

The back should be level, neither dipping nor roaching, and the loin should be short and strong. The hindquarters should be muscular and powerful, and should not 'fall away', that is slope sharply to the tail. The ideal tail carriage is level with the back, or just above it, and it should not curl. When held down, the tip of the tail should reach approximately to the hock.

The neck should be of good length, though a short backed dog will naturally have a proportionately shorter neck than

one with a long back. It should be clean and free from throati-
ness. A really short neck is invariably associated with straight
shoulders, that is with insufficient angulation between the
shoulder-blade and upper arm, which restricts the front movement. The tips of the blades (the withers) should be fairly
close together. Too wide a space between the blades usually
leads to 'bossy' shoulders and too wide a front altogether,
though a Golden is not meant to be a narrow-chested dog. It
should be moderately broad, and also deep in brisket.

The croup should not be too short. Without sufficient length
there, the dog will not have the correct balance, or length and
freedom of stride when moving. When the croup is very short,
it frequently slopes too sharply. The ideal short-coupled Golden
is one that has the correct shortness in loin. In fact no point
in the standard should be exaggerated. A Golden should be
powerful but not over-heavy, head should be broad, but not
coarse, ribs well-sprung, but not covered with layers of fat,
body deep, but not so deep that it is too close to the ground,
making him look too short in the leg. On the other hand,
lack of depth will often make him look too 'leggy', but a
Golden nearly always continues to deepen in body until he is
three years old or even more.

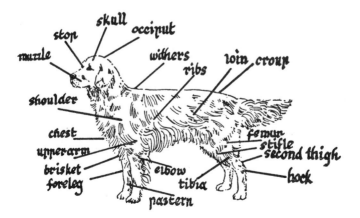

The height is measured from the withers to the ground, There are quite a number of oversize Goldens, but I have only once seen one below the minimum height. Many that are described as being too small, are found, when measured, to be well above the minimum required.

The standard is the description of the ideal Golden Retriever, but it must be remembered that no dog, not even the most famous champion, is perfect.

CHAPTER 2

Choosing a puppy

IF POSSIBLE go and choose your puppy yourself. If you cannot do this, and you don't know of a breeder, write to the Kennel Club, who will give the name and address of one. Write to the breeder stating exactly what you want. You mustn't expect to get a show quality puppy very cheaply just because you only want it as a pet, and are not interested in showing.

Let us suppose you are going to choose your own puppy. He should be sturdy, fairly plump, but he should not have a distended stomach, which is a sign of worms or bad feeding. He should have bright eyes, a clear skin, and should be gay and friendly. If you arrive to see the puppies shortly after they have been fed, don't expect them to be very lively, because they will be much too sleepy. Puppies always play for a short time after their meal, and then have a good sleep. Try and arrange with the breeder the most suitable time to call.

Choosing the best puppy from a litter is not easy, even for an expert, but an experienced breeder has a much better chance of picking the right one. Therefore, if you want your puppy for show and breeding, go to a kennel known for producing winning stock. This is not necessarily the largest, or the one breeding the most litters during the year. Go to some of the championship and big open shows, and talk to the breeder whose winning stock you most admire. Most breeders are only too glad to help you find a really good puppy, and if they haven't a suitable one in their own kennels, will be able to tell you where to get one, probably sired by the stud dog you have been admiring at the show. They will usually help you choose your puppy.

If you have decided to choose your own puppy without help from anyone, then study the preceding chapter on the standard very carefully. Go and see the litter at eight weeks old and watch them very closely running about, and then examine them individually on a table. Decide on the one which is nearest to the standard, as far as that is possible in a young puppy. One point to remember is that the colour of a Golden at eight weeks is lighter than its colour as an adult. Its ears will show the colour it will probably be at maturity.

Before you leave with your puppy, make sure you have the pedigree and if possible the registration certificate, and a signed transfer form to send to the Kennel Club to record the change of ownership. If the registration has not yet been returned by the Kennel Club, then the breeder will send it on to you, together with the transfer form.

Most breeders register their litters, but if you find yours is not registered, write to the Secretary, The Kennel Club, 1–4, Clarges Street, Piccadilly, London, W.1., and ask for form 1A. Before returning it to the Kennel Club, make sure you have obtained the breeder's signature.

If you want your puppy trained for the gun then go to a Kennel where the dogs are worked. Most Goldens will work if given the opportunity, but, as in all breeds, some are better than others, and the best chance of your obtaining a really good Gundog is from working parents.

CHAPTER 3

Rearing and Feeding

WHETHER your puppy is intended for show, work, or just a companion you will want him to grow into a strong and healthy dog, and he won't do this without correct feeding. When you buy your puppy, find out from the breeder exactly how he has been fed, and continue with this, at least for the time being. If you wish to change to some other method, it can be done gradually. A complete change of food on top of a change of surroundings would be upsetting for your puppy.

Methods of feeding can be roughly divided into two: orthodox, and what is called 'Natural Rearing'. Followers of the former may give the meat raw or cooked, but it is usually mixed with biscuit or bread soaked in stock or gravy. In natural feeding as many raw foods as possible are used and meat is never cooked. The meat and biscuit are never fed together, and biscuit meal (which must be wholemeal) is never soaked in meat stock. Other whole grain cereals, such as barley flakes and oat flakes are also used and fed as a separate meal, soaked in milk, vegetable water, or a vegetable extract such as marmite. I feed my dogs in this way, and find it very satisfactory. Herbs and plants are used to provide extra vitamins and minerals, and garlic, which is an internal disinfectant, is given as a prevention against disease and worms. All my dogs have garlic tablets regularly, and they are extremely effective. I obtain these tablets and the other herbs, which are dried and specially prepared for dogs, from Denes Veterinary Herbal Products Ltd., 24 Holbein Place, London, S.W.1. I recommend anyone who is thinking of going in for Natural Rearing to write to them or a similar firm for their puppy feeding charts and other literature on the subject. There is not room here to go into it fully.

Whatever the feeding method, a growing puppy needs a good supply of vitamins and certain minerals, the most important being Vitamins A and D and calcium and phosphorous for forming good strong bone. Cod liver oil and halibut oil are rich in vitamins A and D, and the best source of calcium and phosphorous is bone meal. Naturebone, obtained from Denes, is excellent. There are also some very good preparations on the market which combine all the essential vitamins, minerals and trace elements. One of these is Vivomin, made by Crookes and obtainable from most chemists. If Vivomin is given no other additions to the food are necessary. Other widely used products are Vetzyme, Kenadex and Stress, made by Phillips. These three together provide all the essentials.

As long as it is well-balanced, and the food is of good quality, an adult dog should need very few additions to his diet, the exceptions being stud dogs, and bitches in whelp or nursing a litter. During the winter, I think it is a good idea to give a course of one of these preparations, especially to shooting dogs, who work hard during the season. For the rest of the year, good food should be all that is necessary.

An eight weeks old puppy should be fed five times a day, changing to four times at three months, three times at five months, and twice at nine months. I think it is better to keep to two meals a day for the rest of the dog's life, giving the biscuit meal in the morning and the meat by itself in the afternoon. If possible, two-thirds to three-quarters of the total weight given each day should be meat. Tripe or fish can be given as a change from meat. Fresh herrings are excellent. Meat is better fed raw than cooked, but if kept in a refrigerator, thaw it out before feeding. Add chopped parsley, or grated carrot to the meat sometimes, or garlic instead of giving it in tablet form. The morning meals should consist of wholemeal brown bread or wholemeal biscuit meal soaked in vegetable water, marmite or milk. The latter should be diluted with water for adult dogs, but not for puppies. Biscuit meal should be soaked for an hour before feeding. As a change, give brown bread slices baked hard in a slow oven, or dry biscuits. The 'Natural Rearing' firms make several varieties of good biscuits, and some called milkwheat biscuits, which are great favourites with my dogs, are made by Roberts & Co. (Dunchurch) Ltd.

The average amount of food required each day by a Golden is about 1½-lbs. dry weight, but it varies considerably with individual dogs. As with humans, some can eat as much as they like and still remain thin, while others get fat on practically nothing at all. Young dogs should have more food than the older ones. For instance, a nine months old dog puppy will probably need 1½-lbs. of meat, and ½-lb. cereal food (biscuits, meal, bread, etc.), with a bitch a little less. Stud dogs, bitches in whelp and with a litter, and working dogs during the shooting season all need more meat than the others. Bitches tend to put on weight as they get older, so don't overdo their starch ration. Also with a youngster that is getting too heavy, reduce the starch meals rather than meat. The dog's condition will tell you if you are feeding him correctly.

Inoculations

Followers of Natural Rearing do not have their dogs inoculated, but unless you intend to keep strictly to this method it is safer to have your puppy immunised against Hard Pad and Distemper. This can be done at eight weeks, but many Veterinary surgeons advise waiting till he is thirteen weeks old. Until your puppy has been inoculated don't take him out in the road, or let him mix with other dogs. There are several vaccines, which give protection against Hepatitis as well as Distemper and Hard Pad with just one injection. Another combined vaccine gives protection against the two forms of Leptospirosis. Leptospira Canicola is sometimes called Lampost Disease because dogs catch it through sniffing infected animals' urine. It is quite common amongst town dogs and often leaves the kidneys permanently affected even though the dog recovers from the actual disease. Leptospira Ictero-haemorrhagiae (jaundice) is carried by rats, so is more common amongst country dogs.

Minor Ailments

Golden Retrievers are a hardy breed, and if properly looked

after, are very rarely ill, but all breeds have occasional minor ailments.

ECZEMA can be treated by dabbing the affected parts with calamine lotion, or T.C.P. several times a day. Substitute fish for meat for a few days and give a course of Yeast tablets, such as Vetzyme, which are rich in Vitamin B1.

DIARRHOEA. If your dog has diarrhoea, take him off all solid food for twenty-four hours. I give a mixture of Tree Bark food (from Denes), honey, milk and water, and usually find the dog back to normal by the next day. If, however, the diarrhoea persists, or your dog is listless, off his food, or his eyes are dull, send for your Veterinary Surgeon. They may be symptoms of something more serious and the sooner treatment is started, the sooner your dog will recover. In some cases, particularly with the virus diseases mentioned above, delay could prove fatal.

Another effective treatment for diarrhoea is Kaolin. Buy some Kaolin powder from a chemist, and fill a medicine bottle almost to the top. Add water slowly, shaking the powder down, until the bottle is full, and give a teaspoonful four times a day to a young puppy, up to a tablespoonful to an adult.

You will find your dog will frequently eat grass, especially in the spring when it is fresh and green. He will usually seek out the couch grass, which helps to rid the intestines of worms and other irritants. Do not worry if he eats grass until he is sick. It is just a natural way of ridding his stomach of anything which might be causing him slight discomfort. Persistent vomiting is another matter, and expert advice should be sought at once.

EYES can be kept clean with warm water and cotton wool, but should your dog have a runny or bloodshot eye, such as can sometimes be caused by cold winds, bathe with Optrex, or put in a drop of 5% Argyrol solution. This can be obtained at any chemist.

CANKER. If your dog shakes his head, holds it on one side, and has a brown discharge in his ear, he has canker. A drop of Oteryl massaged into the ear, and then very carefully wiped out with a clean rag will usually clear this up. Otodex and Ryotin are also good remedies.

Severe cases of any of these troubles, or ones that do not yield quickly to treatment, should be seen by your Veterinary Surgeon.

If you suspect that your dog is off-colour, take his temperature. Vaseline the silvered end of a thermometer (the blunt-ended type), and insert it gently into the rectum. A dog's normal temperature is 101.4°, but a few points above that is no cause for alarm. Keep the thermometer in for at least a minute and if it registers over 102° it is wiser to seek professional advice.

Grooming

With regular grooming a Golden doesn't need bathing very often. Most of them love water, and if they go swimming often enough, baths are hardly ever necessary. There are several dry cleaning powders and spirit shampoos which are quite efficient.

I use a good stiff bristle brush for grooming, with a small plastic one for the feathering, and a steel comb. A few minutes daily should keep his coat in good order.

Even a well-cared for dog can sometimes pick up fleas from such things as hedgehogs, so if your Golden scratches examine him carefully. If you find even one flea, powder him all over with one of the products specially made for dogs. Lorexane is one of the best, as it has a much pleasanter smell than some of the others. Get rid of the fleas as soon as possible as your dog can get tapeworm from them. If he drags himself along the ground on his hindquarters don't jump to the conclusion he has worms. He may have, but it is more likely that his anal glands need attention. These two glands are situated either side of the rectum, and need squeezing out occasionally in most dogs. It is a job you can do yourself, but until you have learnt the correct way to do it, take him to your Veterinary Surgeon. If these glands are full it can prevent your dog from being in first class condition, so if his coat is dull, or keeps coming out when it should be growing make sure they don't need emptying.

Golden Retrievers are a long-lived breed, and it is quite usual for them to live till they are fourteen years old, and I have known them reach the age of fifteen and sixteen. Sensibly treated your Golden should give you many years of companionship.

Ch. Camrose Fantango

PLATE I

Dorcas Timberscombe Topper

Ch. Colin of Rosecott, age ten years

Westley Frolic of Yelme

Ch. Alresford Advertiser

Photo: Fall

Photo: King's Photographic Service

Ch. Boltby Skylon

PLATE II

Ch. Weyland Varley

Photo: Fall

Photo: F. W. Simms

Ch. Simon of Westley

CHAPTER 4

Training

THE FIRST two lessons your puppy should learn is to be by himself in a room, and to be clean in the house. He will have been used to sleeping with his brothers and sisters all round him, and if he is suddenly shut in a strange place by himself at night, he will most probably cry very loudly. Sometimes a puppy will settle down without making a sound either the first night in his new home or any other night, but it is just as well to be prepared.

Give him a box just big enough for him to lie in comfortably and some warm soft bedding. Make three of the sides of the box too high for him to climb over. If possible, partition off a corner of the room like a child's playpen and put the box in there, covering the floor with newspaper. In this way any messes will be confined to one place and on newspaper. It also has the advantage of keeping the puppy near his bed. If he wakes in the night and wanders about a strange dark room he will be bewildered and possibly frightened and almost certainly cry.

Give him a good meal in the evening, and when you put him in his pen give him a nylon bone to chew, or a shin bone. I don't recommend rubber bones as the puppy usually manages to get small pieces off and swallows them, and never give chop or poultry bones or any that can possibly splinter. A shin bone will usually keep a puppy occupied for a long time, and one of my puppies would play for hours with a nylon bone.

Put your puppy in his box by himself for short periods during the day, so that he gets used to it. If you keep him with you all day and then leave him alone at night, he is much more likely to make a noise.

If your puppy arrives at his new home late in the day, I

should advise taking him up to your bedroom for the first night. Confine him to a small space near your bed. Take him for a good run in the garden last thing at night, cover the floor with plenty of newspaper and you should have very little trouble. If you do not wish to do that, then try and arrange for the puppy to arrive early in the day, so he has more time to get used to the place where he is to sleep. Alternatively, you could buy two puppies, so that they would keep each other company!

In house training, prevention is better than cure. Don't wait until the puppy has made a puddle on your best carpet, then smack him, and snatch him up to put him outside. He won't have the slightest idea what is wrong. If he connects the scolding with anything at all it will be the act of relieving himself and not the place in which he does it. Take him out at regular intervals and make a fuss of him and praise him when he does what is required outside. Take him out immediately he wakes up, after food, and if he appears restless. Remember that a young puppy's bowels should act after every meal.

Goldens usually house-train very quickly. The first puppy I had only made one mistake in the house. Since I have been breeding, the dogs don't come into the house until they are several months old, and then they are automatically clean, and don't need any house training. However, just occasionally a puppy refuses to be clean at night, although perfectly all right during the day. Don't expect an eight-weeks-old puppy to go through the night without relieving himself, but after a few weeks he should be able to. The best remedy is to put him into a bed at night that he can't get out of. A deep box with wire netting over the top, or turned on its side so that he can see out, will make a suitable bed. Make sure he has plenty of room to lie down comfortably and turn round. It is very unlikely that he will soil his bed, and a few nights like that will probably break the habit.

From a very early age your Golden will pick things up and carry them about. Encourage him to bring them to you. Take whatever he has very gently from his mouth, saying 'dead' as you take it, praise him, and then give it back to him. If it's something you don't want him to have, then give him something else to carry in its place. If he thinks you are going to take everything away from him, he probably won't bring anything to you. Never snatch anything from him or pull it if he is holding on to it, or you may make him hard-mouthed. If he refuses to let go, gently pull his jaws apart, and praise him, when he gives up what he is holding. It is not a good idea for any gundog breed to play 'tug-o'-war', which seems to be a popular game for children to play with puppies.

It should also be impressed upon children that a puppy is not a plaything, though it can be an ideal playmate. It needs plenty of rest, and when it lies down to sleep it should be left in peace until it is ready to play again.

I've never found any of my Goldens resented having anything taken away from them, and I've always been able to do anything to them or for them. However, I suppose there are always exceptions, and if your puppy growls or even snaps when you want to take something from him, you must be firm about it from the start. Never give in to him even once. Sometimes it is only necessary to speak severely to him, but if he persists, a sharp tap on the nose should be sufficient.

Before you take your puppy for a walk in the road, get him used to a collar and lead in the house or garden. The first step is to put a small collar on him. He will try to scratch it off at first, but he will soon get used to it. Then attach a lead to the collar and let him run about like that. Finally, pick up the lead, call him to you, and walk a few yards with him. Gradually increase the distance, until he is quite used to the feel of the lead, and then he is ready for a short walk.

For his first few outings take him to as quiet a road as possible. His first sight of a car coming along the road towards him will probably frighten him a little. In any case, he will almost certainly sit down and watch it pass. Don't pull him on, but stop and stroke him and talk to him until the car has passed. He will soon get used to the traffic and take no notice of it. Gradually introduce him to a busier road until crowds and heavy traffic don't worry him at all. This applies especially if you live in a town, or intend to show your dog, but even if you live in the depth of the country I think it is a good idea to accustom your dog to changes in environment.

Don't take a young puppy for long walks. An adult Golden will walk as far as you like, but when you first take your puppy out, walk him just for a few minutes, gradually increasing it until he is old enough to take all the exercise you can give him. Although plenty of exercise is a good thing, it is not necessary to walk a Golden miles every day to keep him in good health. A brisk walk on the lead on hard ground, and then a good gallop on grass is the ideal. Regulate his food to the amount of exercise he has.

Most Golden Retrievers love cars. Take your puppy on short journeys first, so that he isn't sick. Then when you want to take him a long distance, he will be used to the motion of the car, and it won't upset him at all. If you have to take him on a long journey before he becomes accustomed to the car, give him a travel sickness pill (Shaws make one for dogs), but that should rarely be necessary. I've always found Goldens particularly good travellers. Mine travel hundreds of miles and often sleep in the car as well. They never seem to get tired of it. It is a great asset to have a dog, who will stay happily in the car for as long as you like. It means that you can take him with you to a great many places, which would otherwise be impossible.

CHAPTER 5

Training to the Gun

THIS SUBJECT can fill a whole book, but here I will deal with the elementary training. The first two lessons, to walk to heel and to sit should be taught to any dog whether he works or not. Always make the lessons brief, and don't try to teach too much at once. End the training session when your dog has done something well, so that you can praise him before taking him indoors or returning him to his kennel. If you go about it in the right manner he will thoroughly enjoy his training.

To teach a dog to walk to heel, take the end of his lead in your right hand and hold it behind your back. Then with your left hand, hold the lead near his collar and pull him in close to your left side, saying 'heel' and walk forward briskly. He will probably pull forwards or sideways. Each time he does, say 'heel' and pull him back into position. For a dog that persistently pulls sideways, walk close to a fence or hedge so that there is just room for him to walk at your left side. If he keeps getting too far forward push him back with a stick held in your right hand. I do *not* mean hit him with it, but push it against his chest until he is back in position. After you have done that several times, it should only be necessary to hold the stick in front of him and say 'heel' for him to go back to the right position of his own accord. When the command 'heel' is sufficient to make him walk in the right position try the same exercise off the lead.

Many dogs walk to heel better off the lead than on it, but if your Golden won't come in close enough, pat your leg with your hand as you say 'heel', and stroke and encourage him when he comes to you. Every time he gets too far forward, turn round and walk in the opposite direction, repeating the command as you turn, so that he has to catch up to you instead of being continually checked. Goldens are quick to learn and should walk to heel after a very few lessons.

For the 'sit', place one hand on the hindquarters, and with the other hand push against his chest until he is in the sitting position, saying 'sit' as you do it. Stroke him and praise him while he is sitting and then let him get up. Repeat the exercise until he sits on command. Raise one hand as you give the command. Then try moving a few paces away, repeating the word 'sit' and raising your hand if he moves. Go back to him, and praise him if he has remained in position. Increase the distance you move away until you can go out of sight without his moving, and go back to him each time rather than calling him to you. That will come later. When this lesson has been learnt thoroughly your dog should obey immediately, either when you say 'sit' or when you raise your hand. The latter is useful when silence is necessary as it is sometimes out shooting.

For retrieving, make a dummy by stuffing an old sock and sewing up the ends. Later on the dummy must be made heavier, so that it is nearer the weight of game, and it can be covered with a rabbit or hare skin. Make your puppy sit, then throw the dummy a short distance. Don't let him go for it immediately, or you will encourage him to 'run in'. After a few seconds, point in the direction of the dummy and say 'Get out'. If you have followed the advice in the previous chapter he will probably bring it straight back to you. If he does, hold him under the chin and stroke his head before taking the dummy. This is to guard against his dropping it too soon. He may try to rush past you, but don't let him. As soon as he is level with you, stop him and stand in front of him before taking the dummy. Never snatch it as he passes. If he doesn't bring it straight back, crouch down and call him. This nearly always encourages puppies to come to you. Never run after him, but rather run away from him which is more likely to make him come. Don't just call his name when you want him to come, but say 'Bruce' (or whatever his name is), come', or 'come here'. You will sometimes want to say his name to attract his attention before giving other commands and you will not always want him to come towards you when you say his name.

If he persists in running off with his dummy, take him to a narrow passage, where he can't get out. Sit him at one end and throw the dummy to the other. He will then have to bring it back to you, or stay at the other end of the passage. He will most probably do the former, but if not you will have to use a check cord. Get about fifteen yards of strong, but light cord and attach it to your dog's collar, keeping the other end in your hand. Throw the dummy and send him for it. As soon as he picks it up draw him towards you with the cord, calling him and encouraging him as you do it. When he reaches you, hold him under the chin and praise him before taking the dummy. Repeat this until he comes to you without being pulled in, and then try without the cord attached. When he retrieves to hand properly, keep increasing the distance you throw the dummy and throw it in long grass and other cover, so that he has to use his nose and not his eyes to find it. While he is hunting for it say 'hielost' to him. Make sure he watches you throw the dummy, and throw it up in the air to encourage him to mark. A good marker is invaluable in the shooting field. Get him used to retrieving from bushes, hedges, ditches and brambles.

The next step is unseen dummies, but don't make these too difficult until you have taught direction and control. You will probably have used one particular place for your training, so, throw out a dummy there, and then bring out your dog. Use the same procedure as for 'seen' dummies, make him sit, point in the direction of the dummy, say 'get out', and encourage him to hunt by saying 'hielost'. If he won't go far enough, walk up with him towards the dummy, encouraging him all the time. When you see that he winds the dummy, run back towards the place from where you sent him, and praise him when he brings the dummy to you. Once he has found a dummy that he hasn't seen drop, he will get the idea and hunt better next time. At first all dummies should be upwind, that is with the wind blowing toward the dog. Later he must learn to retrieve downwind, when he has to get out beyond the dummy before scenting it.

The next step is to be able to direct your dog to the place

you want him to hunt. You will need a whistle, which is high-pitched. Many people use a so-called 'silent' whistle. The pitch is so high that it sounds very faint to human ears, but dogs are said to be able to hear it a mile away. The simplest way to work your dog on the whistle is to blow one long blast when you want him to stop and several short blasts in rapid succession when you want him to come to you.

I take my whistle when exercising puppies before starting any proper gun-training and I find a good many of them will come when you blow short blasts without being trained to do so. If your dog doesn't do this, call him by name, and when he is coming towards you, blow the whistle. Praise him when he gets to you. Do this several times and then he should come to you on the whistle alone. If this method doesn't succeed, then use the check cord, whistling as you draw him towards you. If this lesson is learnt before your dog does any serious retrieving, you are unlikely to have any trouble with his return. Whistle him as soon as he picks up the dummy, and he will most probably bring it straight to you. Whistling often speeds up dogs inclined to be slow on the return and so does walking away from them as they are coming back.

If your dog has learnt to sit when you raise your hand, it should be easy to teach him to sit when you blow one long blast on your whistle. Simply raise your hand and blow at the same time. First of all do this when he is close to you, so that if he doesn't obey you can push him into the sitting position. Then send him a few yards away, and increase the distance until he will sit anywhere as soon as you blow a long blast on the whistle. Later on he will just stop and look at you for directions, but until he gains experience make him sit when you whistle.

To teach direction, sit your dog in front of you and facing you and throw one dummy to his right and one to his left. He will want to go for the one you threw last, so make him go for the other one by pointing, and taking one or two steps in that direction and saying 'get out'. If he goes in the wrong direction blow your whistle. If he has learnt this previous lesson properly he should sit at once. Re-direct him, and if he still goes the wrong way, call him back to you. Point to the correct dummy and walk towards it, saying 'get out'. When he has retrieved that dummy send him for the other one. Repeat until he goes in which ever direction you send him the first time.

Next, throw one dummy to one side and the other straight out in front of you, and proceed as for the left and right dummies. Next, try three dummies, so that you can direct him either to the right, left or straight out. When he will go in whichever direction you send him, sit him by your side and throw two dummies out in front of you at an angle and about twenty yards apart. Send him for the one you threw first, and if he starts to go towards the wrong dummy, stop him with your whistle immediately before he gets too near it, and direct him to the correct dummy. If he still goes towards the wrong dummy whistle him back towards you, and redirect him from just in front of you. If he gets to the wrong dummy don't stop him bringing it or you will probably confuse him and spoil his 'pick-up'. Let him retrieve it, and then start again. When he is proficient at this you can direct him on to unseen dummies. Notice which way the wind is blowing and direct your puppy so that the wind blows the scent towards him.

Most Goldens love water, and don't need much encouragement to swim. Try and get your dog used to it before he is twelve months old, even if it's only retrieving a dummy across a shallow stream at first. I had two dogs who only loved water as long as their feet were on the ground. I cured them both by waiting for a warm day and going in swimming myself. They followed and never refused to swim again. In fact they loved it. That is rarely necessary, and if your puppy won't swim at first, he will usually follow an older dog in. For the first swim try and find a place where he can walk in. If a puppy plunges straight off a bank into deep water before he knows what it's all about, he will go right under and that will put him off swimming.

One important thing a puppy should learn at an early age is that he mustn't chase game or livestock of any sort. If possible, take him (on a lead at first, of course) amongst chickens and sheep, and if he pulls towards them, pull him back sharply and say 'No'. The command 'No' should be given any time your puppy is doing, or is about to do anything you don't want him to. He will very soon learn what it means. Even if he looks as if he wants to chase anything, say 'no' very firmly.

If you have room, make a rabbit pen with some bushes in it. Have some tame rabbits and walk your puppy at heel amongst them, make him sit while they run about. Then put him on the check cord and let him run about in the pen, keeping a firm hold on the end of the cord. He will put up a rabbit out of one of the bushes and probably start to chase it. Blow your whistle or shout 'no', whichever he is more likely to obey. If he stops, praise him and call him back to you. If he continues to chase, as soon as he has reached the full length of the cord, throw your full weight against it, and repeat the command on the whistle. The dog will be checked very forcibly and may even fall over, which won't hurt him in the least, but should give him a sharp lesson in steadiness.

When he is reliable, make him retrieve dummies from the pen, and say 'no' if he even looks at the rabbits. Soon he should bring his dummies out of the pen without taking the slightest notice of the rabbits.

Do not let a puppy jump very much because his bone will still be soft, but at about six months in order to teach him what he must do later on, put a barrier of some sort, about a foot high, across a gateway. Leaving him on one side, walk away slowly, calling him and saying 'over'. He will probably just scramble over the first time, but he should soon learn to jump over. If he just sits down and cries and won't get over the barrier, don't lift him. Put a lead on him, and step over the barrier, pulling him up and over at the same time. I've never known this method to fail and can be employed to get your dog over much higher jumps. An adult Golden should be able to jump a five-bar gate with a pheasant in his mouth without any difficulty. Always say 'over' when you want your dog to jump. Then he shouldn't waste time looking for a way through a fence when there isn't one near.

Before firing a gun close to your dog, make sure he is not worried by shots he hears at a distance. Accustom puppies to noises when they are very young. I always clap my hands loudly at a litter of puppies when they are about six weeks old. Most of them just stop whatever they are doing and look at me with interest, but occasionally one runs away into a corner. If a puppy does that, he may be nervous of gunfire, and must be introduced to it very gradually. With any puppy, it is better not to be in a hurry to fire over him. Get a starting pistol and fire it at feeding times, some distance away at first, gradually getting nearer. Then change the pistol for a gun, but before you fire the gun by the puppy's side, take it with you on a training session. Put it over your shoulder, then on the ground next to your dog, so that he is used to the sight of it. When you consider he is ready to be fired over, get somebody else to fire the shot while you stand by your puppy, ready to reassure him if he shows any sign of fear. If he does, fire again, a little bit further away, throw a dummy and let him 'run in' to it. The desire to retrieve will usually overcome his nervousness. If, however, he is really gun-shy, it will require unlimited time and patience to cure him. It can be done, but it really needs an expert to do it.

To start your puppy on retrieving game, try and get a cleanly shot partridge, which is 'cold', but recently killed. Many puppies retrieve their first bird by the wing, so to avoid this put a rubber band round the wings. If a partridge is unobtainable, the next best thing is a small hen pheasant. Pigeons are not very good because their feathers come out, and a mouthful of feathers may put a puppy off. If he won't pick up the bird, put it gently in his mouth, and hold it there, making a fuss of your dog. Throw it a little way and let him run in to it, praising him a lot when he brings it. All the lessons learnt with the dummies can now be repeated with game, and in addition teach your puppy to follow the line of a 'runner'. The collection of wounded birds is a gundog's most important function.

To do this, tie a bird in the middle of a long cord. Take one end, and have an assistant at the other and drag the bird between you, not too far the first time. Loose the bird from the cord and walk back well away from the 'line' of the dragged bird. You want the puppy to follow the scent of the bird and not that of his owner. The puppy must not see you do this, but now bring him out and direct him to the start of the line. In the shooting field this would be the 'fall'. If he picks up the scent and follows the line to the bird, don't interfere with him at all. Only if he doesn't pick up the trail, but ranges all over the place, should you help him with any command or directions. If he doesn't seem to get the idea at all, put him on the lead, take him to the fall, and keep him on the line until he comes to the bird.

The first time you take your dog out on a full-scale shoot, go without a gun, so that you can concentrate entirely on him. If possible, take an older, trained and rock-steady dog with him, and just let the puppy retrieve a few birds. Even if he is used to retrieving cold game, a very soft-mouthed puppy will sometimes have difficulty with freshly shot birds, but with plenty of encouragement and more experience, he will soon get over it. Even if you can't take an older dog with him on his first day, don't give him too many birds to retrieve, as a puppy's first shoot is an exciting and tiring experience. It will do him a lot of good to watch experienced dogs work.

In some parts of the country there are training classes run specially for novices and one-dog owners, though many more experienced people regularly start their puppies at these classes. The United Retriever Club has classes in the Midlands, Bucks, Hants, Kent and Essex, and hopes to start more classes in other parts of the country. The South Eastern Gundog Society has classes in Surrey. At these you will meet many other people interested in training their dogs. There are experienced trainers to help you with any problems that may arise, and your dog learns to work amongst other dogs, and knows that he must sit and watch them working until it is his turn. Both clubs also run tests. It is well worth attending these classes.

You may never have the opportunity to take your Golden out shooting, but don't let that prevent your training him, even if it's only with dummies. You may not have time to teach him the finer points, but let him hunt for and retrieve something. Let him use his nose and his brains and his natural instinct for working. When you see how much he enjoys it, you will find it's well worth while, and I think you will enjoy it too.

CHAPTER 6

Kennels

THE IDEAL for a Golden is to live in the house. If you intend to have just one dog and keep him alone in a kennel, then don't have a Golden Retriever. However well you look after him, he won't be very happy without the companionship of either humans or other dogs. In fact I think it is wrong to keep any dog in that way. If, however, you intend to breed and have several Goldens you will need suitable kennels.

If you are lucky enough to have stables or similar brick buildings these can be converted very easily. Loose boxes don't really need any alteration, except that bitumastic covering on the floor is an improvement. It is damp proof, warmer and much easier to clean than the usual stable flooring. It is, however, rather expensive, so if you leave the floors as they are, or have cement, put down plenty of duck boards for the dogs to lie on.

If you have no out-buildings which can be converted, buy a good wooden kennel. These are usually built of tongued and grooved match boarding, which after a time is inclined to shrink, owing to the difficulty of obtaining properly seasoned wood. This makes the kennel draughty, so it is a good idea to line it with hardboard. It is better to have a separate sleeping compartment, or even a day and night kennel. The bed should measure at least 4-ft. by 3-ft., for two dogs. It should either be a bench with a board in front to keep the bedding in, or a deep box. The best bedding is wheat straw or wood wool, and there should be sawdust on the floor. In summer, sawdust can be used for bedding as it is cooler. The day compartment or kennel should be as roomy as possible, with plenty of sawdust on the floor. It is the best thing for drying kennel dogs, though for obvious reasons, it is no good for house dogs. A wash leather rung out in lukewarm water is ideal for cleaning wet and muddy dogs before going into a house or car. When using sawdust, rub plenty of it well into the coat, and when the dog shakes it out, most of the moisture will have been removed. The front of the dog kennel should have iron bars, so that it can be open in fine weather, and shutters that can be put up in wet weather. If possible have it facing South. An ordinary wooden or asbestos shed can be used as a kennel providing it is well built and has windows.

If your dogs sleep in stables or other lofty buildings in winter, give them a bed which has a top on it. Although Goldens are a hardy breed, and can stand any amount of cold, I don't suppose they enjoy sleeping in an icy cold atmosphere. In an ordinary box, even a deep one, a large proportion of the dogs' body heat will be lost. I use unlined kennels, measuring approximately 5-ft. by 3-ft., inside stables for sleeping quarters. These small kennels are easy to make, or can be bought quite reasonably. I prefer the sort that have both the door, and the iron-barred "window", which should have movable shutters, in the front of the kennel. These can be shut right up in the daytime, when the dogs have large boxes full of sawdust to lie in. In this way they can come in wet and muddy and dry off in the sawdust, instead of making their bedding damp and dirty. Never let dogs go to bed wet. It doesn't hurt them a bit to be wet all day, as they often will be out shooting, providing they don't sit around in a cold wind while they are wet, and are thoroughly dried before going to bed.

I have another kennel measuring 10-ft. by 5-ft. It is made of asbestos with a wooden floor and the walls lined with wood half way up. The box is at one end with a "roof" of hardboard in a wooden frame over it. This can be removed in hot weather, and in very cold weather a sack or rug can be hung in front of the box to keep more of the cold air out and the warmth in.

Runs can be of iron railings, or more usually chain link fencing, which should be buried six inches in the ground, or cemented in. The height of the run should be at least six feet. Runs can either be grass, brick, cement or cinders. The last named are very good except that they get dusty in very dry weather, and make a Golden's coat rather dirty. Bricks are inclined to sink in places, which encourages puddles to form, otherwise they are very good. Cement is the easiest to keep clean, but dogs shouldn't be allowed to lie on it if it's damp. In fact they should be given duck boards to lie on, whatever the surface. Probably most people have grass runs, which are quite satisfactory except in very wet weather, when they get very muddy at gates and round the edges where the dogs walk most. A thick layer of sawdust helps to dry up the mud. Goldens love the sun, but make sure there is adequate shade in summer.

Make the runs as large as possible. Goldens will play together even when they are quite old, and so will get additional exercise that way. Be careful about kennelling two stud dogs together. I have always done it without any trouble, but it could lead to a fight if they play too roughly together. Goldens are not fighters, but stud dogs of any breed are often more "touchy" than bitches or dogs not used at stud. They should be able to be exercised together anyway, or kept together in the house, but I don't advise keeping three stud dogs together however placid and good tempered they are. It might be quite all right, but it's better not to take risks, unless you can keep an eye on them, and stop them if they start playing too roughly.

Keep the kennels and runs clean. Remove any excreta every day, and change the bedding when it gets broken and dusty. Always have clean water available except for about an hour after feeding. Don't leave food in the kennels. Clear away any that is not eaten, and if necessary offer it to the dog later on, but don't leave it lying about.

Don't leave your dogs shut in their kennels for hours and expect them to be clean. Let them out at regular intervals whatever the weather. How often this is necessary depends on individual dogs, and you will have to find out from experience. Amongst my own dogs, one who is in the house doesn't need to go out between 3 p.m. and 10 p.m. or even later, while another is let out about every three hours, except at night, of course, when all my dogs are shut up from 10 p.m. till 8 a.m. When in the house, this bitch has always been clean, but at one time soiled her kennel every night. I cured her by shutting her

Sleepy

Colour photos by Anne Cumbers

Safety doors on a station wagon

Golden Retriever at work

Golden Retriever whelping box

Golden Retriever puppies

Golden Retriever : Heron Vale Destiny

At home in the country

A bowl for each puppy in this litter

right up in one of the small kennels at night with her kennel companion. This usually works, as not many dogs will soil their bed. There are a few exceptions, and the best way to cure these is to use the same method that I recommended in an earlier chapter. Shut the dog in a box just big enough for him to lie down and turn round comfortably for a few nights. This should break the habit.

To sum up, before building or converting your kennels there are three points to consider:

(1) Careful planning.
(2) Combining comfort and healthy conditions for your dogs. They need plenty of light and air, so never shut them in kennels without windows.
(3) Easy management.

CHAPTER 7

Care and Preparation
of the Show and Working Dog

LOOKING after a Golden you wish to show and work is not very different from caring for any other dog, but certain points, such as the right sort of exercise, need special attention. Sufficient road exercise is essential to bring a puppy up on his toes and to keep the feet a good shape and the nails short. A dog who has all his exercise on soft ground has to have his nails cut. The combination of trotting on hard ground and galloping on grass should develop all the muscles properly. Opinions differ considerably as to how much road exercise is necessary. Mrs. Charlesworth advocated four miles a day for a puppy of six months, increasing to six to eight miles a day with a bicycle by the time he is twelve months old. Although one must respect such an opinion it is an open question whether this amount of exercise is necessary, and I personally don't now know of anybody who takes his Goldens six or eight miles on the road every day either with or without a bicycle. With big runs to play in, and additional exercise off the lead on grass, two miles a day on the road should be sufficient. An older dog, already in hard condition can be kept that way with less than two miles.

It does, however, vary with different dogs. If you have one that doesn't play and spends most of his time lying about, or one that is inclined to get fat and heavy then he will have to have more exercise. It is not necessary to take him with a bicycle, though it is an excellent way to harden up a dog that is in soft condition. If he is not used to bicycle exercise take him a short distance at first. A very good way to strengthen hindquarters is to make your dog keep running up a steep slope. Throw a dummy to the top for him to retrieve. Be careful of allowing him to retrieve a ball, unless it is very large a dog may swallow it and choke to death.

A dog that works during the shooting season should have regular exercise for the rest of the year. If he is just allowed to potter about all the summer you can't expect him to go straight out and do a hard day's work without getting tired. I don't believe it is necessary to keep a working dog very thin. He certainly shouldn't be fat, but he can be kept in hard condition without looking all skin and bone. Increase his food while he is working, though some dogs will get thin in spite of more food especially young ones. As long as he has plenty of meat and extra vitamins it won't matter. For the show ring, your Golden should be nicely covered without being fat. His body should be shapely, and not look exactly the same from shoulders to quarters.

A dog loses his coat once a year, and a bitch more often, depending on her seasons. She will usually come into season as she is coming into full coat, though this does not always happen. A Golden right out of coat is at a great disadvantage in the show ring, although it is a temptation to take him if he has been entered. He never looks so bad at home as he does when he gets into a ring full of dogs in beautiful coat. Brush and comb all the dead hair out to encourage the new coat to grow quickly. Denes seaweed powder is excellent for improving the coat and making it grow more quickly.

Before taking him to a show, your Golden will need a little trimming to make him look tidy and show his true outline. Start with his tail which should have about four inches of feathering at the root tapering to a point at the tip. Cut it the right length with sharp scissors and then neaten it with a trimming knife. The tool I use for trimming is a stripping knife, but many people prefer the type which is a small comb with a razor blade attached. Most good dog shops will have both in stock. The feathering on the hind legs shouldn't be touched except to trim the long ends just above and below the hocks. The hair which sometimes sticks up between the toes should be trimmed off with the knife and then the rest of the foot done with scissors. Long hair left on the feet makes them look the wrong shape. The feathering on the front legs shouldn't need much attention, but if it gets too long trim it with the knife. Don't use scissors. Trim the long rather woolly hair that grows on and behind the ears, and take off the hair that sticks out either side of the neck. Some Goldens grow a lot of thick long hair on the neck, shoulders and chest, and in this case, the careful use of thinning scissors will help to give a smoother look. Then trim the long ends with the knife. If possible get somebody to show you how to trim your Golden, but if nobody is available remember that the whole object is to tidy the dog and not to make him look like a shorn lamb, and the marks of scissors or knife should not be obvious. Trimming, particularly the tail, is better done several days before a show.

Although bathing is not necessary if the dog is clean, I think most Goldens look at their best after a bath. Ordinary soap can be used, but I think one of the shampoos specially made for dogs is better, especially with hard water. I find Shaws Double Strength Insectidal Shampoo is excellent, and makes the coat really shine. Except for very unruly coats which are probably better done two or three days before, bath your dog the day before the show. Rinse him well and take him outside to shake and run about. Then partly dry him with a clean wash leather or rough towel. While he is still fairly wet the coat must be combed into position. In warm weather, and if you have time, comb him dry in the sun. In colder weather it can be done in front of a fire or with a hair dryer. If you don't do this, tie a dry towel over him to keep the coat fairly flat. If left to dry on its own pieces of hair will probably stick up in all directions. In cold weather don't put a dog straight back in a kennel after drying him by the fire. If possible keep him in for the night, but, if not, when he is quite dry, take him for a walk before returning him to his kennel.

Before taking your dog to a show give him some ring training. Some Dog Training Clubs hold classes for this, which have the great advantage of getting your dog used to a ring full of other dogs. If there is no Club in your area, you can at least teach your dog to trot by your side without pulling forwards or sideways. When the judge asks you to move your dog, you must take him at a trot straight away from the judge to the other side of the ring, and straight back again. He mustn't gallop or leap about. Train him to stand still while the judge is looking at him. A tit bit in your pocket is very often a great help for this, but not all dogs are the same, and you have to find out the best way to make your dog show. If you can do it without touching him, so much the better. In some breeds, the exhibitors get down on their knees and hold up their dog's head and tail. There is nothing to stop your showing your Golden in this way if your particularly want to (though some judges won't have it), but very few Retriever exhibitors do 'top and tail' their dogs, and to my mind nothing looks nicer than a Golden standing four-square on a loose lead, with his tail wagging and his eyes fixed on his handler. If you can't get your dog to look alert in this way, and not all of them will, then try and train him to stand reasonably still. Sometimes a hand under his chin will have the desired effect.

Make sure your Golden, if it is a male, is entire. That means that both his testicles have descended into the scrotum. Monorchids, which have only one testicle descended, or cryptorchids which have both testicles retained in the abdominal cavity, are not eligible for shows. Many novices, who know nothing about this rule, have had the disappointment of being turned away at the entrance to the show by the Veterinary Surgeon, whose job it is to examine the dogs for these defects, and to see that the dogs have no sign of any infection. Give your dog a garlic tablet daily for a week before and after the show to help guard against infection. Even if you never go near a show, I recommend the regular use of garlic. Your dog is just as likely to pick up infection from another dog who is running about the roads as he is from shows, where the dogs have been vetted before being allowed in.

These, then, are the points to remember when preparing your dog for showing, correct feeding, the right amount and the right sort of exercise, grooming, trimming and ring training.

CHAPTER 8

Shows and Field Trials

THERE ARE five types of shows held under Kennel Club rules.

1. EXEMPTION SHOWS. These are the only shows at which dogs that are not registered at the Kennel Club may be exhibited. They are usually run in conjunction with a fête or flower show, or in aid of some charity. There are four classes for pedigree dogs only and usually several novelty classes, such as the best conditioned dog, or the one with the most soulful eyes. Any dogs, pedigree or mongrel, can enter these. Entries can be taken at the show and cost from 1/- to 2/6 a class. The prize money varies considerably.

2. SANCTION SHOWS. Small shows of twenty classes, confined to members. There are not many breed classes, and you would probably have to enter a class such as Any Variety Retriever, or Any Variety Gundog. No dogs which have won a challenge certificate are eligible, and the highest class is Post Graduate, i.e. for dogs which have not won more than four first prizes, each of the value of £1 or more in post graduate, minor limit, mid limit, limit and open classes. Entries close about a fortnight before the show, and fees are usually 3/- per class and prize money, 10/- for 1st, 5/- for 2nd and 3/- or 2/6 for 3rd. The show is not benched and the dogs sit around the hall.

3. LIMITED SHOWS. Although these are confined to members and are limited to dogs who have not won a challenge certificate they usually have more than twenty classes, and may have any classes including open. The entry fees and prize money are usually higher than sanction shows, and there are some breed classes, so you may have one or possibly two for Golden Retrievers.

4. OPEN SHOWS. These are open to all dogs and all

exhibitors. They are usually benched, though some of the smaller ones are not. They vary considerably in size and you may have just two classes for Golden Retrievers (probably novice and open) or ten classes with the sexes divided. Entry fees usually 6/- for non-members and 5/- for members and prize money £1, 10/- and 5/-. Entries close two to three weeks before the show.

5. CHAMPIONSHIP SHOWS. These are the most important shows of all. They are held in different parts of the country and people come to them from all over the British Isles. Prize money is usually £2, £1 and 10/-. Entries may be 12/- per class and 3/- benching fee, or they may be on a sliding scale such as £1 for the 1st entry and 10/- for each subsequent entry with no benching fee. Entries close about four weeks before the show. These are the shows at which champions are made. Kennel Club Challenge certificates are awarded, one for each sex, and to become a champion a dog must win three challenge certificates under three different judges. In Golden Retrievers and all other Gundog breeds it is necessary to obtain a qualifying certificate at a Field Trial as well as three C.C.s to become a champion. This rule was brought in to preserve the working instinct in Gundogs and without a qualifying certificate the dog is allowed to take the title of Show Champion (abbreviated to Sh. Ch.). Challenge Certificates are awarded to the best of each sex provided that in the opinion of the judge the dog is worthy of the title of champion. If there is no dog that the judge considers is worthy of that title, then he must withhold the C.C. In all the years that I have been showing this has never happened in Goldens, but it has in some other breeds where the standard is not so high and the number of entries much smaller. The total number of entries and of dogs runs into thousands at Ch. Shows, and the more breeds classified, the higher the entry. Cruft's offers C.C.s to every breed eligible for them, and that is over 100 breeds. In 1961 they had a World record entry of 15,721 made by 7,502 dogs. The smallest Ch. shows have an entry of between 2,000 and 3,000.

Golden Retrievers have certificates at all the twenty-two

General Ch. Shows, and in addition have two Breed Club Ch. Shows, one run by the Golden Retriever Club, and the other by the Northern Golden Retriever Association. A breed show is really the best place to bring out a puppy to his first show. It is less crowded and quieter. Failing that, a small open air show is the best, but do try to avoid a very crowded show in a small hall unless your puppy is very used to crowds of people and dogs.

If you want to enter for shows and don't know of anyone to tell you when they are being held, order a weekly copy of *Our Dogs* or *Dog World* or preferably both. Not only will they advertise all the forthcoming shows but they contain many interesting articles and news of your breed. Having selected the show you wish to attend write to the Secretary for a schedule. Once you have exhibited at a particular show you will be sent schedules for all their future shows without applying for them. When you receive the schedule, make a note of the date entries close, as any received after that date will be returned. At the larger shows there are any number of different classes, some governed by age, such as 'puppy' for dogs over six months but not over twelve months, 'junior' for dogs between six and eighteen months old, etc. Others depend on the dog's previous wins, such as 'novice' for dogs who have not won a C.C. (Challenge Certificate) or three or more first prizes (puppy and special puppy classes excepted), or higher up the scale, 'mid limit', for dogs which have not won three C.C.s, or five or more first prizes in all in mid limit, limit and open classes. Class definitions vary slightly between championship and other shows, but they will be clearly set out in the schedule, so if you read them carefully you shouldn't make any mistakes.

If you have a puppy that hasn't won anything, or only won in puppy classes, then you can enter him in any class you like. At big shows you may have puppy, junior, maiden and novice in your breed, which would be suitable. If there is no Golden Retriever puppy class then try Any Variety puppy. Fill in the entry form carefully giving your dog's full registered name. A few days before the show you will receive an exhibitor's pass for you and your dog to enter the show.

Get to the show in good time, so that your dog can settle down before going into the ring, and you have time to groom him properly. Have a show bag into which you can put everything you want to take to the show. You will naturally need a brush and comb, and a dish for water. I always take a bottle of water with me as the tap or tank for water is sometimes a long way off. Take a rug, or plenty of newspaper for him to sit on if its a benched show and a rug is useful at an unbenched show too as the floors are often dirty. Take your exhibitor's pass, a safety pin for your ring number, a collar and lead, or a collar and bench chain for a benched show, and a show lead for when your dog is actually in the ring. At the bigger shows there are always stalls selling these leads and chains. A damp wash-leather is excellent for cleaning your dog in wet and muddy weather or if you have to travel by train. If he is very dirty, wet the dirty parts and rub in dry white sawdust, which you can take in a tin or strong bag. If he is due in the ring shortly after you arrive, then use the leather only, or he will not have time to dry properly. Don't forget to take some tit-bits to encourage your dog to show. Well cooked liver is a favourite with most dogs. Except when he is in the ring your dog shouldn't be off his bench for more than fifteen minutes.

Don't be afraid to ask advice at the show if you don't know what to do, but don't select an exhibitor who is hurrying into the ring. A steward will call out when the judging of your breed is about to commence, but just in case you miss the announcement, find out in which ring Goldens are to be judged and keep your eye on it. Be ready to go into the ring when your class is called, as it wastes a lot of time if the steward has to come to fetch you. After you have been given your number, stand with the other dogs that have just come into the ring. Most judges will ask all the exhibitors to move round the ring together. Have your dog on the inside. It is surprising how many newcomers move their dogs round on the outside and so obscure the judge's view of them. Remember your dog has to go at a steady trot. Don't rush round so that he has to gallop or walk too slowly, so that he has to walk or 'pace'. A dog is said to be pacing when he moves both his front and hind leg on the same side forward at the same time. A jerk on the lead will usually make him break into a trot.

The judge will then examine each dog individually and move him straight away and straight back. While the other dogs are being examined let your dog relax, so that he will be fresh and ready to show to advantage when the judge is selecting his winners. As soon as the last dog has been moved make your dog stand as he has been trained to do at home. You may find that in the excitement of his first show he will forget all his training, but don't worry, do the best you can and he will get used to it after one or two shows. If you are called into the middle of the ring keep your dog showing until the judge has marked his judging book.

Don't be too disappointed if you don't get into the cards at your first show. Entries are usually large and competition keen. There is often so little between the dogs that the judge at the next show may prefer your dog to those that beat him previously, or he may show better. If you become a regular exhibitor you will make many friends and see many beautiful dogs so that you will thoroughly enjoy a show whether you win or lose.

As well as these classes for 'beauty' a large number of shows also have Obedience classes and many of the Championship shows have Obedience certificates. A dog becomes an Obedience Champion after winning three of these. Although the best training for Goldens is specialized Gundog training, obedience is better than nothing at all. For an unruly dog a course at one of the many Obedience Training Clubs (the address of your nearest one can be obtained from the Kennel Club) can do nothing but good. Numbers of people take their dogs to these classes to learn how to make them obedient, without entering for any competitions. A dog that is slow at his gundog work may be made slower still by too much obedience, so confine him to the Gundog training classes.

There are also shows confined to Obedience only and Working Trials, which contain tracking and man work, and are mainly for Police and service dogs. A dog can become a Working Trials champion. Every dog and bitch that has won an Obedience certificate during the previous year is invited to compete at Cruft's. No other dogs are allowed to compete and a dog winning the certificate there becomes an Obedience Champion even if he has only won one certificate before. This coveted award was won in 1960 by the only Golden Retriever Obedience Champion, Mrs. K. Needs Castelnau Pizzacato, bred by Miss M. Baker. There are comparatively few Gundogs in Obedience as they have their own specialized form of competition in Field Trials.

FIELD TRIALS

There are different Trials run for all breeds of Gundogs. Some are for Pointers and Setters, others for Spaniels, and the ones we are interested in, the Retriever Trials. Just as there are different types of shows, the same applies to Field Trials.

1. PUPPY STAKES. As the name implies these are confined to Puppies, but the definition of a puppy in this case is different from the one for shows, which is not over twelve months. At trials, a puppy is any dog who was not born before January 1st of the year preceding the trial. For example at a puppy stake held in November 1960, all the competing dogs must have been born on or after 1st January 1959. Thus it is possible to have a 'puppy' that is nearly two years old, or one under twelve months old in these stakes. Very occasionally a club will run a Junior Stake, which is for dogs under two years old.

2. NOVICE or NON-WINNERS STAKES. Definitions vary slightly for these. A novice stake is usually for dogs which have not won a 1st, 2nd or 3rd prize in any stake. The qualifications will be clearly stated on the schedule. Very often there is a Puppy and Non-Winners Stake, which means that as well as the Non-Winners, puppies compete whether they have won at the other trials or not.

3. OPEN STAKES. These are open to all, but there are different types of open stakes. Those run by the Utility Gundog Society are open to any breed of Gundog, though they must work as Retrievers. There are Open Stakes for Retrievers, and most important of all the Open Stakes, which qualify for the Retriever Championship, usually known as Ch. Stakes. Unlike shows, the number of entries for a Field Trial is limited. If

you wish to enter for a trial you send in a nomination and places in the trial are drawn for. A one-day trial is limited to twelve nominations (with a few exceptions, such as the Utility Trials) and a two-day stake to twenty-four. Only Ch. stakes are run over two days. Nominations for nearly all trials greatly exceed the number of places, so some societies restrict their entries for Ch. Stakes to dogs which have won at least a Certificate of Merit at an open stake or a 1st, 2nd or 3rd at a Non-Winners Stake. These trials must then be called All-Aged Stakes, as they are not open to all. As well as the General Field trial Societies which run stakes for Any Variety of Retriever, most of the breed clubs run their own. The Golden Retriever Club, The Northern Golden Retriever Association and the Golden Retriever Club of Scotland all run trials for puppies and Non-Winners and have one stake which qualifies for the Championships. A dog becomes a Field Trial Champion when he has won two stakes, at least one of which is open to Any Variety of Retriever. The dates of all Field Trials are published in the Kennel Gazette obtainable from the Kennel Club.

The Retriever Championships are held each year in December. Every dog who has won a ch. stake is invited to compete, and in a two-day stake the second prize winner is invited as well. Thus you have all the best dogs in the country competing for the supreme honour of winning the Retriever Championships. The winner becomes a Field Trial Champion, even if he only qualified to compete by being 2nd in a two-day stake. Since the war two Golden Retrievers have won the Championships. In 1952 the winner was Mrs. Jean Lumsden's F.T.Ch. Treunair Cala, and in 1954 it was Mrs. June Atkinson's F.T.Ch. Mazurka of Wynford.

A Dual Champion is a dog who has won his title in two spheres, and in Gundogs usually refers to one who is a champion at Show and Field Trials, but it could mean Show and Obedience or Working Trials Champion. An International Champion is a dog who has won his title in two countries, such a dog who becomes a champion here and is then exported to France or America and wins his title there. Eire has its own

Kennel Club, so a dog who becomes an Irish Champion as well as an English Kennel Club Champion also gets his International title. These titles, although widely used, are unofficial, and in Kennel Club records a Dual Ch. would be referred to as Ch. and F.T.Ch. and an Int. Ch. as Ch. and Irish Ch. In Ireland and America champions are made by winning points and not by challenge certificates. Northern Ireland, Scotland and Wales come under our Kennel Club.

Before entering your dog for a Field Trial make sure he is steady to shot, because if he runs in or chases he will be disqualified. It is very difficult to be quite certain that any dog will not chase a rabbit or hare that he puts up when actually out working, though, of course, he shouldn't. You should, however, be able to prevent his leaving your side to go after shot or untouched game. Sometimes a dog who is perfectly steady at home will run in at a trial. There is an atmosphere of excitement and you will probably transmit some of your own nervousness to your dog. Even the old hands feel nervous sometimes, but it is worth every minute of it. Don't be discouraged if your dog doesn't do too well at first. As long as he is fundamentally a good working dog he will do better when both you and he gain in experience.

Before you enter for a trial try to go and watch one, so that you will see how they are run. There are usually three judges and they each have two dogs at a time in the line. Each dog generally has two retrieves under his first judge and then goes out of the line until called in again to go under his second judge. Every dog must go under at least two judges unless he has run in, been out of control, or guilty of hard mouth. If a dog fails to find the bird he was sent for, he is called up and a second dog sent. If this dog finds the bird he is said to have 'wiped the eye' of the first one. A dog may 'wipe the eyes' of several others and he, and those who collect strong runners are likely to be at the top. A dog who has not had the opportunity to 'wipe an eye' or collect a runner but who has done everything that was asked of him efficiently may still get in the awards, and will almost certainly get a certificate of merit.

After all the dogs have been under at least two judges, the

three of them will have a conference and select the best dogs for a run-off. Sometimes one dog has been outstanding and is an obvious winner, he may be 'put on ice' (not asked to do any more) while the others compete for the rest of the awards. At the end of the trial the judges will again confer while everybody else walks back to the meeting place to await the results. Don't forget to offer your dog a drink of water, and dry him well, preferably with a damp wash-leather which will clean him as well and then put him back in the car. All the competitors will be called together to hear the results, and the winner will make a very short speech of thanks to the judges. If you have won an award I expect you will be even more pleased than with your first show award, but if you haven't, don't be too disappointed, keep on training your dog and try again another day.

CHAPTER 9

Breeding

A GOOD MANY people become breeders and exhibitors without setting out to be either. They buy a bitch puppy as a companion. It turns out well, they are persuaded to show it, and it does some winning. They become regular exhibitors, and of course, breed from the bitch and keep a puppy to show as well.

However, let us suppose you are starting from scratch, and intend to breed and show Golden Retrievers. You must decide whether you want to start with an adult bitch, who is already a winner, which would be the more expensive, but the safest way, or a promising puppy, which I think is more interesting. Remember that nobody can guarantee that a young puppy will become a champion and I should be very suspicious of anyone who did, but an experienced breeder who knows what his or her own stock produces will be able to provide you with a puppy that has every chance of turning out well.

Choosing a Bitch

I have dealt with choosing a puppy in an earlier chapter, so now we will suppose you wish to start with an adult bitch. It is unlikely that you would be able to buy a champion or near champion, even if you wanted to, as Golden Retriever breeders can only rarely be persuaded to part with their big winners, but you could probably buy a young bitch, who is ready to start on her show career, or has done a little winning as a puppy. As I advised in the chapter on choosing a puppy, try to have an experienced breeder with you to help you with your choice, but if you have to rely on your own judgment, then I can only repeat, learn the standard and compare the bitch to it. While remembering that no dog is perfect, avoid such faults as an incorrect mouth, cow hocks, a hard, untypical expression and white feet or blaze and anything more than a few white hairs on the chest. If she is free of these faults, has most of the virtues laid down in the standard, is a sound mover, and has the typical friendly Golden temperament with no sign of nerves, ask to see her retrieve. If she has had no training, she will probably run in, perhaps circle round her owner before delivering to hand, or any of the other things mentioned in chapter 5 but as long as she has the instinct to hunt and retrieve, the rest should come with training. See that she comes from a good bitch line, that is a line which consistently produces good Goldens.

Most Goldens are not fully mature until they are about three years old, but they are very good lasters and their show, working and breeding life lasts for many years. Don't expect your bitch to be fully developed by the time she is twelve months old. Those that are, usually become too heavy and their show career finished when others are just coming to their best. Though with a dog it is just a matter of time, a bitch usually matures after a litter, but on no account must you mate her too young just to hasten development. The best age is about two years old. She will probably have her first heat, or season, as it is usually called, at about ten months old, but it can be as early as eight months or as late as eighteen months. The length of time between seasons varies considerably and bitches who come on heat regularly every six months are in the minority. Eight or nine months is quite common and sometimes it is only once a year, specially amongst those bitches whose first season is late. She must be kept away from all male dogs for at least three weeks.

Choosing a Sire

In selecting a sire for your first litter it is as well to choose a dog who has already sired winners and workers. Later on, by all means try out a young dog you like and you think will suit your bitch, but until you gain experience a proved sire is the better.

A dog is more likely to be a dominant sire and produce puppies with his own good points if he is line-bred, that is carrying the same lines on both sides of his pedigree, and if possible the bitch should carry a similar line. There are excep-

PLATE III

Int. Dual Ch. David of Westley

Photo: C. M. Cooke

Left: F.T. Ch. Mazurka of Wynford

Below: Dual Ch. Stubbles-down Golden Lass, F.T. Ch. Stubblesdown Larry, and Ch. Braconlea Gaiety

Photo: F. W. Simms

PLATE IV

Sh. Ch. Waterwitch of
Stenbury and her
daughter Sh. Ch. Water-
sprite of Stenbury

Ch. Sally of Westley

Photo: C. M. Cooke

Ch. Camrose Nicolas
of Westley

tions and sometimes a dog, who is the product of an outcross mating, is a very successful sire. In this case, you will usually find that at least one of his parents was line-bred. A 'chance-bred' dog, however good, is also unlikely to be a good sire. That means a dog who is the only good one in the litter, and who has mostly mediocre ancestors. This also applies to a bitch and that is the reason for starting with one from a good line.

Although line-breeding to first class dogs is the best way to fix the good points in your strain, faults can also be fixed in this way, so don't be afraid to outcross sometimes to improve certain points. Never line-breed to mediocre dogs, or to dogs who do not possess the correct temperament. Remember, too, that Golden Retrievers are Gundogs, and working ability should be taken into account.

Mating

Before mating, your bitch must be in good health and hard condition. You will, of course, have given her the right food, and plenty of exercise. Make sure you know the exact day she comes into season, that is the day she first has a coloured discharge, otherwise it is difficult to decide which day to take her to the dog. If you have male dogs around they will let you know when she is near her season by paying her more attention than usual. Other signs are passing water more frequently and licking herself. It is better to book the sire in advance, and then let his owner know immediately she starts her heat. With most bitches the best day for mating is the twelfth or thirteenth, but some will stand better as early as the tenth day, and others on the fourteenth or even later. If it is a short journey arrange to take her on the twelfth day and then if she is not ready you can take her back and try again the following day, but if it is a long way try and arrange to stay overnight. If it's not possible, at least see that the bitch has some rest after she has been mated. It is always better to accompany your bitch, but if you send her by train, see that the box is large enough for her and is securely fastened. Make quite sure you have the correct train times and notify the stud dog owner well in advance. Get to the station in plenty of time. You have to fill in a form, the bitch has to be weighed and then taken by a porter to the Guard's van. Go with her and see that she is put in a good position, and not in a place where she is surrounded by so many parcels that she doesn't get any air. I've always found British Railways very good with dogs, but I don't take any risks. Never send an 'in season' bitch loose on a collar and chain.

When the time comes for the actual mating, keep your bitch on the lead when introducing her to the dog. Even the best tempered bitch may snap when the dog first tries to mount her especially if she is a maiden. Most stud dog owners will ask you to hold your bitch's head after allowing her a little time to get used to the dog. If she is ready she will turn her tail to one side. While you hold her head firmly to prevent her turning round suddenly, the dog's handler will probably support her under the loin, in case she sits down or twists away suddenly just as the dog is about to tie. She may even try to do this after they have already tied, which could injure the dog, so they should be held until the tie is over. Then the bitch should be returned to the car or kennel and left to rest quietly.

Occasionally you will come across a bitch who really dislikes being mated, and these are usually pet bitches who are not so used to other dogs as those in a kennel. She will snap at the dog, struggle and refuse to stand still. Forced matings should be avoided if possible, so encourage her to play with the dog if she will, and perhaps walk them about on leads for a few minutes. If she still refuses to stand the only way to get her mated is to hold her firmly and muzzle her. Some people won't have forced matings on any account and though I sympathise with their point of view, the fact remains that some bitches would remain unmated for the whole of their lives if they were not held, and some stud dogs would be badly bitten.

If you have a dog you want to use at stud, for his first mating try and get an experienced bitch who is quite ready and willing to be mated. Most dogs know exactly what to do, but if he is hesitant, this sort of bitch will encourage him. If you have a bitch who snaps at him, it may put him off for a time. Try and get your dog used to your supporting the bitch right from the beginning. A stud dog who objects to any assistance is at at a disadvantage with a difficult bitch. Don't let a dog spend too long trying unsuccessfully to mate a bitch. Give him a rest for half-an-hour or so and then let him try again. Sometimes a dog will have difficulty in mating a large bitch and I have found that a piece of sloping ground with the bitch facing downwards is a great help. Even with a small bitch, if the dog is having any trouble a slope seems to solve the problem. I remember that with one of my first bitches I had to stand in a ditch to get her mated!

Don't use a young dog too much at stud. The best age for his first bitch is between twelve and fifteen months. This is generally agreed upon, but opinions differ considerably as to how many bitches he should be allowed to mate before he is two years old. The lowest number I have heard is four, and for a very immature dog, that is probably enough, but with an early developer twice that number is unlikely to do him any harm. If you are training your dog to the gun, it is as well to restrict his bitches severely until he is trained.

Do not feed your dog before he serves a bitch. A few biscuits or a drink of milk won't hurt if the mating is to take place late in the day, but never a big meal. After the mating is over, let him rest in a kennel or the house by himself for a little while before putting him back with other dogs.

The stud fee should be paid at the time of the mating, and is for the actual service and not for the result. However, if the bitch 'misses', that is, fails to have puppies it is the general practice to allow a free service next time the bitch comes into season.

Care of the in-whelp bitch

After a bitch has been mated, and has finished her season, she can return to her normal and regular exercise, but she shouldn't be made to jump, and I think shows are better avoided. Give a garlic pill every day from the day of mating until the puppies are weaned. I never worm my bitches unless they show signs of having them. Adults rarely have round-worms, and if they have tapeworm, segments of it can be seen in the motions. Keep a lookout for this at all times and get rid of it immediately by using one of the many tapeworm remedies on the market or write to one of the Natural Rearing firms for their remedy. Don't wait until the bitch has been mated. There are other forms of worms that adults can have, but their condition will show it, and a Veterinary Surgeon should be consulted.

An in-whelp and nursing bitch should have plenty of meat and milk plus additional vitamins and minerals. It is not necessary to increase the amount of food for the first four weeks of pregnancy when I start increasing the meat ration. For the vitamin and mineral supplements use the products mentioned in the chapter on feeding, that is, Denes or one of the other National Rearing Firms Products, Crookes Vivomin, or those made by Phillips. Directions for use will be given with all these. I also give Denes Raspberry leaf tablets, which are an aid to easy birth.

She should have 1½-lb. of meat a day, or even more if she is the type of bitch who normally eats large meals without getting fat. Give her up to 2-lb. a day. Milk should be given with a raw egg beaten up in it sometimes or thickened with honey and Tree Bark food. Do not increase the starch ration, especially if the bitch is inclined to get fat: A fat bitch is less likely to have an easy whelping. At about seven weeks divide the meals and feed three times a day instead of twice.

Very occasionally a bitch will become difficult over her food when she is in whelp. In this case tempt her with different things until you find something she likes, and remember that it is protein she needs more than anything else. Her protein ration should be increased by at least half as much again as in her normal diet, and I like to increase it by more than that. However, you cannot force a bitch to eat, and the addition of 'Casilan' to her food will give additional protein. Make sure that she gets the vitamin and mineral supplements somehow. If all else fails Denes Naturebone tablets and halibut oil capsules can be pushed down the throat. To do this, open the bitch's mouth, drop the tablet at the back of the tongue and immediately push it down her throat with your finger.

Keep up regular exercise until she gets heavy when she will probably be disinclined to take definite walks on a road but will follow you at a slow pace over fields or if allowed plenty of freedom she may exercise herself but make her take just a little exercise every day. Avoid taking her in the car after about four weeks.

Except in the case of a very small litter, it is usually possible to say that a bitch is definitely in whelp between five and six weeks after mating, but there are other signs before this. In a maiden bitch the teats are often enlarged and rather pink by about three weeks. She usually drinks more water than usual, and very often (though not always) takes great care of herself. She doesn't rush about or play with the other dogs.

Whelping

The period of gestation is nine weeks, but maiden bitches, or those with a large litter sometimes whelp quite safely as much as five days early. Older bitches, and those with small litters frequently whelp late, and some strains invariably do so. I have heard of one bitch who whelped a perfectly normal litter nine days late, but that is exceptional, and I should advise consulting a veterinary surgeon if your bitch has not had her puppies by the 66th day just to make sure that everything is in order. If, before that time she seems restless or ill or has a blackish discharge or if she starts whelping more than five days early then call your vet.

She should be introduced to her whelping quarters a week before she is due. If she is a house dog, let her spend some time there each day. If she lives in a kennel with other dogs, put her in there at night. The whelping box should be about four feet square, with a rail fixed inside, $5\frac{1}{2}$ inches high and about the same distance from the sides of the box. If a puppy crawls behind its mother's back, it can get squashed and suffocated, but the rail prevents this happening, as the bitch can't get right up against the sides of the box. Make the sides about eighteen inches high, and the front should consist of separate boards, which should be movable. Before the bitch whelps leave just one board in the front, so that she doesn't have to jump into the box. After whelping add another board, but don't make it too high to begin with, or she will find it difficult not to jump on to her puppies.

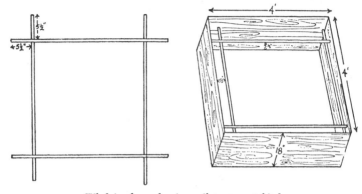

*Whelping box, showing rail to prevent bitch
accidentally suffocating puppies.*

I prefer to have another box for the actual whelping. This need not have a rail round it, as you will be there to see that nothing happens to the puppies. After whelping, the bitch and puppies can be transferred to a clean dry box. Make sure that both boxes are scupulously clean.

With a summer litter, make sure that the whelping quarters are cool enough. In hot weather, a kennel out in the full heat of the sun is unbearable and the puppies get very distressed. In winter, of course, the opposite applies. The quarters should be completely dry and draught-proof and the problem is keeping the puppies warm. Some people argue that Goldens are a hardy breed and as long as they have plenty of straw, puppies need no artificial heat. In my experience, straw gets pushed to the sides of the box, and puppies thrive and are much more contented with an infra-red lamp hung over the box. Use the dull-emitter or those that give a red glow and not the bright ones that are used for pigs. Hang the lamp about three feet above the box, and make sure that it cannot fall down. If no electricity is available, an oil heater can be used, but this must be fixed firmly to the wall, and don't place it too near the box. With a spring litter neither of these problems arise. This is the best time of all, but unfortunately bitches don't

70

always co-operate by coming into season at the most convenient time!

Have plenty of clean newspaper ready for the bitch to lie on while whelping. I find this the most satisfactory, as it can be removed as soon as it gets soiled, and clean paper put in its place. For the second box, to which you move the bitch and puppies after whelping, newspaper is quite satisfactory for the first few days, but after that it gets scratched up by the puppies' feet. A piece of sacking or rug that has been washed and disinfected can then be substituted, but it should be nailed down at the sides to prevent the puppies crawling underneath it. Naturally it should be changed when it gets soiled. A little straw can be put round the edge for extra warmth in winter.

Usually the first sign that a bitch is about to whelp is that she refuses her food. This is not always the case, and some of my bitches have eaten a hearty meal within an hour or two of whelping. The puppies will be carried lower down, the vulva will be swollen and there will be a thick whitish discharge. If you take her temperature, it will be below normal, probably about ninety-nine degrees. Later she will become restless, and start scratching about in her box to prepare a bed for the puppies. If she has the freedom of the garden, she may dig a large hole ready for them. If she does, it is better to confine her to the house or kennel where you can keep an eye on her. Her teats and vulva should be washed with a weak disinfectant solution (Dettol is very good), and then dried with a clean towel. This should be done at the first sign that whelping is near, but in addition to this, I do it several days before she is due, in case she is one of those who gives no sign until the last minute. I have one bitch who behaves perfectly normally until her labour actually commences. She has done this on two occasions, then proceeded to have nine puppies in 2½ hours with the greatest of ease. This is very unusual, but some of them don't give very much warning.

When whelping has begun in earnest, she will pant frequently, turn round to look at her tail and lick herself. Stay with her while she whelps and have a bowl of disinfectant and a clean towel for your own hands.

71

Goldens are very easy whelpers, and rarely need any assistance, but they like to have their owners with them, and enjoy a drink of warm milk every hour or so. Make a note of the time the bitch first begins to strain. If she has not produced a puppy within two hours, call in your Veterinary Surgeon. Usually the first puppy will be born about half-an-hour after the onset of labour. The time between straining will get less and less, and the straining itself become more vigorous until you notice the 'water bag' protruding from the vulva. This contains fluid to aid the birth of the puppy, which should arrive very shortly after the bag bursts. The puppies are enclosed in a membrane, which the bitch will quickly tear. She will vigorously lick the puppy all over and push him about with her nose to get him breathing properly. She will bite the umbilical cord which attaches the puppy to the after-birth, and probably eat the after-birth. Some people prevent their bitches doing this but my bitches always do, and it's never done them any harm. It is the natural thing for them to eat it. Sometimes if the bitch is very large she will find it difficult to get round to attend to her first puppy, or very occasionally a maiden bitch doesn't seem to know what to do. In this case, push the puppy towards her head, and encourage her to lick it. You will have washed your hands in the bowl of weak disinfectant, and if the bitch still refuses to attend to her puppy, break the membrane round the puppy's head, and remove any mucous from its mouth with your finger. The cord should be severed about three inches from the puppy by taking the cord in the thumb and first finger of either hand and pulling with the hand nearest the puppy towards his stomach. Never pull away from the stomach or you will cause a hernia. Put the puppy between his mother's front paws and she will almost certainly lick it and attend to it properly, but if not rub it with a warm dry towel, and then put it where it can feed.

I have never had a bitch who refused to attend to her own puppy, and it is rare for a Golden not to manage everything very well on her own. However, I have on occasions assisted with the birth of an extra large puppy which has decided to come feet first. Take hold of the hind legs, which will be protruding from the vulva, and pull gently every time the bitch strains. Do not pull while she is not straining. Puppies should be born head first, but unless they are very large, they seem to arrive just as easily the other way round.

The length of time a bitch takes to have a litter varies considerably. They may, like the bitch mentioned earlier, have them one after the other very quickly with practically no effort. Sometimes they have about three in the first hour and then an hour or more with nothing happening at all, before they start again. There is no need to worry unless she continues to strain without any result. Always call in a Veterinary Surgeon if she has been straining two hours without a puppy being born.

With a large litter, the puppies born first are inclined to get in the way and get wet all over again as each of the later ones are born, so it is a good idea to have a covered rubber hot water bottle on one side of the box. The puppies can be put round it, and they will often crawl there themselves while their mother attends to the new arrival. I think this is better than putting them in a separate box with a bottle, which might worry some bitches.

Don't forget to give her a drink of warm milk at frequent intervals. Little and often is much better than a large dishful. You can add a little glucose or honey, and if the litter is a large one, or the bitch is in labour a long time, add a teaspoonful of whisky or brandy. Most bitches will lap that up with avidity!

It is difficult to be quite sure when a bitch has finished whelping, but you will probably find that after one or two slight strains to clear herself out, she will clean herself up and then settle down to sleep for a while. If after an hour she seems quite peaceful and there are no more strains, change the puppies into the second box which should be already prepared. If the boxes have to be moved about, it is better to have another person to take the bitch out to relieve herself while you are doing it, or even if you are only changing the bedding in the same box. Many bitches have the annoying habit of whelping in the middle of the night. In which case you may prefer to take her into the kitchen to have her puppies. I nearly always do myself, especially in cold weather as it has the advantage of warmth, good lighting and a stove to heat the milk, and make myself a cup of tea! If you do this make sure the whelping quarters are warm enough before putting the puppies in there, as a sudden big drop of temperature would be dangerous. To transfer the puppies put them in a large basket lined with something warm and cover them over and take them immediately and quickly to their new quarters with the bitch following. Put them at once into the bed, and let the bitch see you doing it. She will get in with them, and if she doesn't, then make her, and stay with her until she settles down. I do this with all my bitches, but if your bitch is a nervous or excitable type, and you think she would resent your picking up her puppies, then let her whelp in her own quarters, and don't handle the puppies more than absolutely necessary.

Once the whelping is over the bitch should be disturbed as little as possible. Give her a drink, dry her 'trousers' a little, but don't wash them, and then let her rest for two or three hours before giving her another drink and taking her temperature which will probably be up a degree or more. Take it night and morning and if it is over 103° the day after whelping, consult your Veterinary Surgeon in case it means a retained after-birth or a dead puppy. Other signs of this are restlessness, renewed straining and possibly neglect of the puppies. The temperature should be normal by four days after whelping.

Most bitches are reluctant to leave their puppies just at first, even to relieve themselves, but they must be made to do so. You may have to put a lead on your bitch to get her out of the box. She will probably have diarrhoea for the first day or two, and should be kept on milk food for the first forty-eight hours. I feed my bitches five times a day on a mixture of Tree Bark food (Denes), honey and milk, which is nourishing and helps to clear the diarrhoea.

Although I have naturally mentioned various things that might go wrong with a whelping bitch, I cannot emphasize too strongly that they very rarely do. In almost every case the whelping will proceed quite normally from beginning to end without any human aid. Once, I came down in the morning to find ten thriving puppies had been born to a bitch who had given no signs whatsoever of whelping the previous night. (Now I take a bitch's temperature when she is near her time.) I don't suppose any breed has a better record of trouble-free whelping than the Golden Retriever.

CHAPTER 10

Care of a Nursing Bitch and her Puppies

A NURSING BITCH needs plenty of privacy. Keep away other dogs and strange people, and if all seems to be well just go in to feed her and let her out. After 48 hours on milk foods only, give fish for one meal, and add a little brown bread or cereal flakes to one milk meal. On the fourth day increase the amount of fish and cereal food. On the fifth day when her temperature and bowels should be normal, give one meal of meat. By the end of the week she should be having 2-lbs. of meat a day, given in two meals. Four meals a day should be given altogether. First thing in the morning give Tree Bark, milk and honey, or milk thickened with a little Farex. Give the meat meals about mid-day and 4 p.m. and milk at night with wholemeal biscuit meal, brown bread or cereal flakes. The vitamin and mineral supplements should be given until the puppies are completely weaned. Add a raw egg to one meal about three times a week. A nursing bitch needs plenty of food, but naturally the amount varies with the size of the litter. A normal litter is about eight puppies, but Goldens frequently have more than that. The largest number I have heard of is fifteen, but that is unusual, and it is never wise to let her rear more than ten. Either have a foster mother or harden your heart and put the weakest down. Some people will tell you that you shouldn't keep more than eight puppies, but I have known many bitches rear ten without any trouble at all.

If the litter is large she can have more than 2-lbs. of meat and an extra meal can be given, making it five a day. If the bitch seems very hungry then give her more food, as the demands made on her will increase with the puppies rapid growth. Most bitches can safely be given all they will eat. From the third day after whelping give a daily garlic pill.

Examine her milk glands every day because if the puppies are not feeding from all the teats those left out will become congested. This is very likely to happen with a small litter. The gland will feel hard and lumpy and should be massaged. Milk the teat and then put a puppy to feed from it. Encourage the puppies to feed from any gland that has been congested. Soiled feathering can be cleaned with a damp wash leather and the very soiled pieces cut off. In cold weather, cut off as little as possible, as feathering keeps the puppies warm.

If you have an infra-red lamp raise it slightly during the day so as to keep the temperature as even as possible. The puppies should be gradually hardened off, by first of all raising the lamp, then turning it off at the warmest part of the day, then all day, and eventually off altogether by the time they are ready to go to new homes. Puppies start to open their eyes at about nine days old, but they are not properly open until they are a fortnight. Until then the Kennel should be kept fairly dim. Later on, of course, plenty of sunlight is good for them, but in warm weather do be sure that they can get into the shade.

At a fortnight old or before, if they are long, their claws should be cut, or the bitch will be badly scratched. Cut just the tips with sharp scissors or nail clippers and be careful not to cut the quicks. After that cut the claws once a week.

Weaning

Puppies can usually get all the food they want from their dam until they are four weeks old, but it is a good idea to teach them to lap at three weeks old. Heat some milk until it is just warm and put it in a thermos flask, or it will be stone cold by the time it is the turn of the last puppy. Put the puppies, one at a time, on a sheet of paper and put a little milk into a saucer and dip the puppy's nose into it. Hold the saucer up to the puppy rather than push his nose into the milk. Some will lap straight away, but others will just sit there with their chins resting on the saucer, and some will blow bubbles. Do this again the next day and you will find that most of them will lap quite well. Always wipe the milk off their mouths afterwards.

The best thing for weaning puppies is goats milk, but nowadays it is not easy to get. It is particularly good thickened with honey and tree bark food and the puppies love it. Unpasteurised Jersey milk, prepared the same way is also quite satisfactory, but again that is difficult to obtain. Owing to these difficulties, most people, except those who have their own cows or goats, and the strict followers of Natural Rearing, use one of the milk powders specially prepared for puppies. If you have to bottle feed a puppy for any reason, a milk powder which has the ingredients of bitches' milk in the correct proportions is the best. If the dam's milk is inadequate and the puppies are not thriving, buy a premature baby's feeding bottle and give them supplementary feeds from that. I have never found this to be necessary, but I have hand-reared a terrier puppy that was turned out by his mother at 24 hours old. In this I was helped by my first Golden Retriever, Simon, who not only kept him warm and clean, but licked his tummy after every meal, as the puppy's mother would have done to help his bowels and bladder function normally. Without the help of a canine nursemaid, it is essential that the puppy's tummy is massaged with cotton wool soaked in olive oil, and it has to be fed throughout the night as well as the day, so hand-rearing puppies is quite hard work.

With a normal sized litter at three weeks give the puppies one meal of milk with tree bark and honey if it's goat's or cow's milk, every day, so that they are lapping really well by the time they are four weeks old. If they don't look fat and sleek and well nourished give them two or more meals but you will rarely find it necessary. At four weeks give them a teaspoonful of scraped raw meat. Roll it into a ball and hold it to the puppy's mouth. He will probably eat it at once, but if he doesn't, open his mouth gently and put a little meat in it. I've never known a puppy refuse it after he has once tasted it. Also at four weeks add a few brown bread crumbs or raw barley flakes to the milk meal, and give an extra meal of plain milk and Farex. Increase the amount of meat every day until they are having an ounce and three milk meals by the time they are five weeks old. Give them each a garlic pill every morning and start them on the extra vitamins and minerals at this age. Half the way through the sixth week give an extra meat meal, so that by the time the puppies are six weeks they can be independent of the bitch altogether. From five weeks the meat can be cut up very small instead of scraped, and the size of the pieces gradually increased.

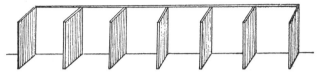

A useful partitioned feeding box for puppies.

Always feed puppies individually and not from one large dish, or the greediest will get more than their share. A good way to prevent them taking each others food is to get a long board and fix partitions to it. Put the dishes between the partitions and put one puppy to each dish. After a time the puppies usually run to their own dishes but watch that the quickest eaters don't try and 'help' the slower ones after they have finished their own! Gradually increase the amount of food at each feed until at eight weeks old they are having four ounces of meat twice a day, an early morning meal of ¼-pint of milk, tree bark food and honey, and two other meals of ¼-pint of milk with Farex, brown bread, flakes or puppy meal. These are average amounts and can be increased if the puppies look thin, or decreased if their stomachs bulge too much after food. Overfeeding will often cause diarrhoea. When using meal soak it for one hour before feeding. Always use wholemeal, and a very good puppy meal is made by Roberts & Co. (Dunchurch) Ltd., Dunchurch, Rugby. They also make hound meal. Offer the puppies fresh water every day but don't leave it down in a run with them. They will only paddle in it and probably turn the dish upside down. They should be wormed at six weeks old. Garlic given daily will gradually rid puppies of worms, but it is sometimes a slow process and it is better to worm them before they are sold, which is usually at about eight weeks old. Write to Denes for their worm mixture or get some Banocide, made by Burroughs Wellcome. This is very safe and doesn't upset the puppies, but always be careful to give them the correct dose.

For the first few days after her puppies are born the bitch will stay in the box with them the whole time, and her food should be held for her to eat there. Later she will be outside the box for short periods after she has fed the puppies. She should have a bench or something to lie on, out of reach of the puppies when they come out of the box, which should be at about three weeks old. Until then all the movable boards in front of the box should be in position to prevent the puppies climbing up and falling out on to the floor where they would get very cold especially if just one climbs out and so has none of the others to keep him warm. When it is time for the puppies to come out of their bed, remove all the boards in front, so that they can just walk out. Have sawdust on the floor, and they should then learn to keep their bed clean.

Once you start feeding the puppies take the bitch away from them for a short time at first and then for increasingly longer periods. Always feed the puppies before she goes back to them. Even if they have just had a large meal, they always seem ready to feed from their dam, but if they have just fed from her they will be disinclined to eat the food you give them.

When the puppies are about five weeks old the bitch will probably vomit up her food for them. Allow them to eat it, but give her some more food, and see that she doesn't have large lumps of meat or the large hound meal which would be most unsuitable for the puppies even though it will be partly digested when she brings it up. At this time, I feed my bitches on puppy meal rather than the larger size meal, and cut up their meat much smaller than usual. Brown bread or flakes are also quite all right. Some bitches will go on feeding their puppies until they are three months old and others are only too glad to be rid of them at six weeks old. I always put a bitch in with them at night until they are seven weeks old, but she must be able to get away from them. I strongly suspect that a good many of them jump straight on to their own bench and only get down when the puppies are asleep, but until six weeks I think a bitch should be made to stand still for the puppies to feed last thing at night. After that I let her do as she likes but whether she feeds them or not the puppies should be having five meals a day. From the end of the fifth week start to decrease the bitch's food so that her milk dries up gradually and she keeps in good condition as the puppies feed less and less often from her.

At eight weeks, a puppy can be safely sent on a train, and can do without food for up to twelve hours. Give him a good meal of raw meat before he starts on his journey. If he has to cross London and you can't take him to the London station yourself, arrange for someone to meet him, and take him across to the other station. There are people whose business is arranging the transport of dogs and they will undertake to do this and to feed him if necessary. See that his travelling box is large enough and has sufficient air. Apart from ensuring the puppy's comfort, British Railways are not allowed to accept dogs for transport in unsuitable boxes. The puppy must be able to sit straight up without his head touching the top and he must have plenty of room to lie down and turn round. Don't, however, go to the other extreme and send him in a box that is much too big. Send a diet sheet on ahead of him, so that his new owner can have the correct food when he arrives. Always give a 'diet sheet' with every puppy you sell. Have all your pedigrees written out by the time your puppies are ready to go. It is very disappointing for anyone who comes to buy a dog to be told that his pedigree is not ready and it will be sent on later. If he is registered hand the new owner the registration card and a signed transfer form. The Kennel Club usually sends a supply of these forms when returning the registration cards. When registering a whole litter, a special litter registration form should be obtained from the Kennel Club. If you intend to breed several litters take out your own kennel suffix, which can be used as a prefix, before every name, or as an affix, such as my own 'of Westley'. Once registered, a dog's name may not be changed, except by the addition of another prefix or affix, should the dog change hands. Without your own kennel name, it is very difficult to think of different names for all the puppies and ones that have not already been used. It costs £2 to register a prefix with the Kennel Club and 10/6 a year to maintain it, or a payment of five guineas will maintain it for life.

If you intend to breed Golden Retrievers, right from the start aim to produce the dual-purpose dog, the good-looking worker who can win at shows, the show dog who can hold his own in the shooting field and win at trials. One of the most coveted awards is that of the Gold Trophy presented each year at Cruft's to the best Golden Retriever who has won at Field Trials. You may have disappointments, but when you succeed, and you will if you persevere on the right lines, you will think it has all been worth while.

Perhaps you do not yet own a dog. Do you want a faithful companion, good tempered and devoted to children, hardy, and adaptable, or a show dog easy to prepare and handle in the ring, or a gundog, who, if he is bred right will be easy to train, keen and persevering, good in water and in the thickest cover? Perhaps you want all three. Then you want a Golden Retriever.

Interesting details about the Golden Retrievers whose photographs appear between pages 32-33 and 64-65

The records of these dogs are correct to July 1st 1961

PLATE I. The Golden Retrievers pictured here are chiefly famous for the success of their progeny though the three dogs have themselves gained top honours:

Champion Camrose Fantango (Born 1951). By Dorcas Timberscombe Topper ex Golden Camrose Tess. Owned and bred by Mrs. Joan Tudor. His chief win was best of breed at Crufts in 1956. He won the Alison Nairn Stud Dog Progeny cup for five years in succession (1955–9) and was runner-up in 1954. This cup is awarded each year to the dog whose progeny wins most points at shows and field trials, and a similar cup is awarded for brood bitches. Fantango's winning sons and daughters include three champions, as well as other C.C. winners and overseas champions. His dam, Golden Camrose Tess (one C.C.) was the foundation bitch of the Camrose Kennel. She was the dam of two champions, and has many champion and C.C. winning descendants.

Dorcas Timberscombe Topper (1946–58). By Dorcas Bruin ex Timberscombe Trefoil. Owned by Mrs. Elma Stonex and bred by Mrs. Joan Cousins. Winner of two C.C.s. Sire of five champions, winner of the stud dog progeny cup in 1953 and '54 and runner-up twice. Mrs. Stonex also owned Ch. Dorcas Glorious of Slat (1943–55). By Dorcas Bruin ex Stella of Slat, bred by Mrs. Pope and winner of four C.C.s. He won the stud dog cup in 1950, '51 and '52, and was runner-up in 1953. He sired three champions and two Field Trial champions (one of them an International Dual Champion). Both these dogs have an enormous number of winning descendants.

One other dog who won the Stud dog cup three times in succession (1947, '48 and '49) was Mrs. M. Thompson's (Pennard) Stubbings Golden Nicholas, who was bred by Mrs. Nairn.

Champion Colin of Rosecott (1946–59). By Sh. Ch. Roger of Rosecott ex Dawn of Rosecott. Owned and bred by Miss Rosemary Clark. He has sired six champions, which is the highest number by a post-war Golden and also three other C.C. winners. He won four C.C.s himself.

Westley Frolic of Yelme (1946–60). By Simon of Brookshill ex Lively of Yelme, owned by Miss Joan Gill and bred by Major H. Wentworth-Smith. She won the brood bitch cup for four years in succession (1954–7) and was the dam of three champions, another C.C. winner and many other winners.

PLATE II. These dogs have won the highest number of C.C.s amongst the post-war Goldens:

Champion Alresford Advertiser (Born April, 1951). By Ch. Alexander of Elsiville ex Ch. Alresford Mall. Owned and bred by Mrs. Lottie Pilkington. Winner of 35 C.C.s under 29 different judges, the highest number ever won by a Golden Retriever, and also field trial awards. He has won reserve best in show (all breeds) at Ayr Ch. Show and best in show at The Golden Retriever Club Ch. Show and Northern Golden Retriever Association's Ch. Show. He is also a winner of the coveted Gold Trophy at Cruft's. This is the trophy awarded to the best Golden having won at Field Trials. He has sired a champion, a show champion, several other C.C. winners and overseas champions, and has several times been runner-up for the stud dog cup.

Champion Boltby Skylon (Born July, 1951). By Boltby Kymba (two C.C.s) ex Boltby Sweet Melody. Owned and bred by Mrs. R. Harrison. Winner of 29 C.C.s under 23 different judges. He has won best of breed at Cruft's two years in succession and at the Northern Golden Retriever Association's Ch. Show three times. Sire of two Show Champions and some overseas champions. His sire, Boltby Kymba, also

sired Ch. Boltby Moonraker, who himself sired three champions and two Show Champions.

Champion Weyland Varley (1949–59). By Weyland Venturer
ex Ch. Culzean Sulia. Owned by Mrs. H. J. Morgan and bred
by Mrs. Porter. He won 14 C.C.s under 12 different judges
and was best in show (all breeds) on the first day of the Three
Counties Ch. Show and Reserve best in show both days. He
was a Field Trial winner and sired several Field Trial winners.
He was a Cruft's Gold Trophy winner.

Champion Simon of Westley (Born April, 1953). By Ch.
Camrose Fantango ex Westley Frolic of Yelme. Owned and bred
by Miss Joan Gill. Winner of 21 C.C.s under 21 different
judges. His Field Trial awards include a first prize. He was
Reserve Best Dog in Show (All breeds) at Birmingham
National Centenary Ch. Show. He won the Cruft's Gold
Trophy for four years in succession and has been best in show
at the Golden Retriever Club Ch. Show. His winning progeny
include two C.C. winners, two Field Trial first prize winners
and overseas champions, and he has been runner-up for the
stud dog cup.

PLATE III. Except for Ch. Braconlea Gaiety, the dogs on this
page are chiefly famous for their work at Field Trials, though
two of them are dual champions, and another a C.C. winner:

International Dual Champion David of Westley (Born June,
1951). By Ch. Dorcas Glorious of Slat ex Ch. Susan of
Westley. Owned by Miss Lucy Ross and bred by Miss Joan
Gill. He is the only International Dual Champion there has
ever been in the breed, being a Champion and Field Trial
Champion and an Irish (Eire) Champion and F.T. Champion.
He has won four C.C.s, eight Green Stars (Eire) and, trained
and handled by Mr. Jim Cranston, 24 Field Trial awards,
including a diploma in the Retriever Championships. He has
been runner-up for the Rank-Routledge Cup, which is awarded
each year to the Retriever (any variety) who wins the most
points at Field Trials. He won the most points at trials in
1955 amongst the Goldens. He won the stud dog progeny cup

in 1960, and sired Mrs. C. R. Hutton's Ch. Dai of Yarlaw (also a Field Trial winner) and several Field Trial winners including Mrs. Margaret Barron's Moonbeam of Anbria, the Golden who won most Field Trial points in 1960. Moonbeam's dam, Miranda of Anbria, is the third generation 'Anbria' bitch champion. David's dam, Ch. Susan of Westley who won the C.C. and Cruft's Gold Cup in 1948, had another champion son, and several champion and Field Trial winning descendants.

Field Trial Champion Mazurka of Wynford. (Born April, 1952). By F.T. Ch. Westhyde Stubblesdown Major ex F.T. Ch. Musicmaker of Yeo. Owned and bred by Mrs. June Atkinson. Winner of five open stakes, this outstanding Field Trialer won the Retriever Championship in 1954, was runner-up in 1955, and won the Rank-Routledge Cup in 1957. He is the sire of Mr. Martin Atkinson's F.T. Ch. Holway Zest (who was second in the Retriever Championships in 1959) and other Field Trial winners. His sire, Westhyde Stubblesdown Major, was bred by Mr. W. Hickmott, and owned by Mr. and Mrs. Peter Fraser. He gained his F.T. Ch. title by winning two Any Variety Stakes and while still a puppy won a diploma in the championships. The following year, 1952, he was fourth. This was the year that F.T. Treunair Cala won. Major's tragic death at the early age of two and half years was a great loss to the breed. Mazurka's dam, F.T. Ch. Musicmaker of Yeo, the foundation bitch of the Holway Kennel, was bred by Mrs. Lucille Sawtell. She won 18 awards in trials, she is dam or grandam of numerous Field Trial winners, including four F.T. Champions. Mr. and Mrs. Atkinson train and handle the 'Holways', who have several times won the highest number of points at trials amongst the Goldens.

Dual Champion Stubblesdown Golden Lass (1944–58). By Stubbings Golden Garry ex Stubbings Golden Olympia. Owned by Mr. W. Hickmott, and bred by Mr. F. D. Jessamy (Braconlea). She became the first post-war F.T. Champion in 1948, and the following year won her title at shows to become the breed's first Dual Champion bitch. She is the dam or grandam of five Field Trial Champions and has numerous other Field Trial winning descendants, largely through her two sons, F.T. Ch. Stubblesdown Larry (by Ch. Dorcas Glorious of Slat) and F.T. Ch. Westhyde Stubblesdown Major (by Stubblesdown Riot). In 1952 Lass was awarded the Cruft's Gold Cup, and Mr. Hickmott won it outright, having gained it three years in succession with the three different dogs in this photograph. The Gold Trophy replaces this cup.

Field Trial Champion Stubblesdown Larry (1949–60).
Owned and bred by Mr. Hickmott. He won one C.C. and 23 Field Trial awards. His best win was first in the Kennel Club, 24 dog, two day Open Stake. Int. Dual Ch. David of Westley was third in that stake, so it was a great day for Golden Retrievers. Larry won the Cruft's Gold Cup in 1952 and has many F.T. winning children and grandchildren. He was trained and handled by his owner, as are all the Stubblesdowns except Lass, who was handled by Mr. Jack Curtis. Larry's litter brother, Stubblesdown Ladis, won two C.C.s and a Field Trial award, and sired Mrs. Joan Hendley's Samdor Nimble Nick, who has won two C.C.s and 31 Field Trial awards.

Ch. Braconlea Gaiety (1946–61). By Dorcas Bruin ex Stubbings Golden Olympia. Owned by Mr. Hickmott and bred by Mr. F. D. Jessamy. Winner of nine C.C.s under seven different judges, and a winner at trials. She won the C.C. and Gold Cup at Cruft's in 1950, and was Best in Show (all breeds) at the Three Counties Ch. Show in 1951.

PLATE IV:

Show Champion Waterwitch of Stenbury (1953–60). By Ch. Boltby Skylon ex Bewitching of Stenbury. Owned and bred by Mrs. Enid Minter. She won eight C.C.s all under different judges and was Best-in-Show (all breeds) at Leeds Ch. Show in 1956. Unfortunately died at an early age, but left a show champion daughter and another C.C. winner.

Show Champion Watersprite of Stenbury (Born January, 1957). By Ch. Boltby Moonraker ex Waterwitch of Stenbury.

Owned and bred by Mrs. Minter. Winner of five C.C.s and Best-in-Show (all breeds) at the Three Counties Ch. Show in 1959. Mrs. Minter created a record by winning the Supreme award at a Ch. Show with mother and daughter. The first Golden Retriever to win Best-in-Show at a Ch. Show was Mr. F. Parson's Ch. Torrdale Happy Lad.

Champion Sally of Westley (1949–55). By Dorcas Timberscombe Topper ex Westley Frolic of Yelme. Owned and bred by Miss Joan Gill. Her death at only six and a half was a great blow. She was Best-in-Show at the Golden Retriever Club Ch. Show in 1955 and won nine C.C.s altogether. Sally, Ch. Braconlea Gaiety, and Mrs. Dadd's Show Champion Danespark Angela have all won nine C.C.s, which is the highest number to be won by any post-war bitch. Sally and Angela have won their C.C.s all under different judges, and in 1961 Angela was best of breed at Cruft's and Reserve Best Gundog.

Champion Camrose Nicolas of Westley (Born October, 1957). By Ch. William of Westley ex Camrose Jessica. Owned by Miss Gill and bred by Mrs. J. Tudor. He has won ten C.C.s under ten different judges. He won the C.C. at the Golden Retriever Club Show in 1960 and Cruft's 1961 and was Best Gundog at Manchester Ch. Show in 1960, and Reserve Best-in-Show (all breeds) at Bath Ch. Show in 1961. His sire Ch. William of Westley sired three champions and a Show Champion.

Additions in 1963.

Ch. Camrose Fantango has now sired 5 champions.

Holway Lancer, who is a son of F.T. Ch. Stubblesdown Larry, and grandson of F.T. Ch. Musicmaker of Yeo, has become a F.T. Champion.

Sh. Ch. Danespark Angela now has 11 C.C.s, and the late Whamstead Diana won 10.

Ch. Camrose Nicolas of Westley now has 16 C.C.s and three Field Trial awards. He was Best In Show (all breeds) at Hove Ch. Show, 1962, and won the Gold Trophy at Cruft's, 1963.

Ch. Simon of Westley won the Gold Trophy at Cruft's, 1962, and has now sired 3 C.C. winners and 3 F.T. First Prize winners.

Golden Retriever Clubs

THE GOLDEN RETRIEVER CLUB

Secretary: Mrs. V. G. Till,
Roundwood Kennels,
Cockfield,
Bury St. Edmonds,
Suffolk.

THE GOLDEN RETRIEVER CLUB OF SCOTLAND

Secretary: Mrs. A. Ord,
Douglen,
Nr. Langholm,
Dumfriesshire.

THE NORTHERN GOLDEN RETRIEVER ASSOCIATION

Secretary: Mr. W. D. Barwise,
Waverlea,
Park Road,
Wigton, Cumberland.

For any Gundog breed

THE SOUTH EASTERN GUNDOG SOCIETY

Secretary: Mr. J. K. Childs,
Burghwood,
Bookhurst Road,
Cranleigh,
Surrey.

For any variety of Retriever

THE UNITED RETRIEVER CLUB

Secretary: Mrs. M. Jay,
4, Coldbath Road,
Kings Heath,
Birmingham 14.

Index

INDEX